Oxford Modern Britain   SERIES EDITOR: JOHN SCOTT

Youth and Employment in Modern Britain

The *Oxford Modern Britain* series comprises authoritative introductory books on all aspects of the social structure of modern Britain. Lively and accessible, the books will be the first point of reference for anyone interested in the state of contemporary Britain. They will be invaluable to those taking courses in the social sciences.

Oxford Modern Britain

Youth and Employment in Modern Britain

Kenneth Roberts

OXFORD UNIVERSITY PRESS
1995

Oxford University Press, Walton Street, Oxford OX2 6DP

Oxford New York
Athens Auckland Bangkok Bombay
Calcutta Cape Town Dar es Salaam Delhi
Florence Hong Kong Istanbul Karachi
Kuala Lumpur Madras Madrid Melbourne
Mexico City Nairobi Paris Singapore
Taipei Tokyo Toronto

and associated companies in
Berlin Ibadan

Oxford is a trade mark of Oxford University Press

Published in the United States
by Oxford University Press Inc., New York

British Library Cataloguing in Publication Data
Data available

Library of Congress Cataloging in Publication Data
Data available
ISBN 0–19–827965–5
ISBN 0–19–827964–7 (Pbk)

Typeset by Hope Services (Abingdon) Ltd.
Printed in Great Britain
on acid-free paper by
Biddles Ltd., Guildford and King's Lynn

Foreword

The Oxford Modern Britain series is designed to fill a major gap in the available sociological sources on the contemporary world. Each book will provide a comprehensive and authoritative overview of major issues for students at all levels. They are written by acknowledged experts in their fields, and should be standard sources for many years to come.

Each book focuses on contemporary Britain, but the relevant historical background is always included, and a comparative context is provided. No society can be studied in isolation from other societies and the globalized context of the contemporary world, but a detailed understanding of a particular society can both broaden and deepen sociological understanding. These books will be exemplars of empirical study and theoretical understanding.

Books in the series are intended to present information and ideas in a lively and accessible way. They will meet a real need for source books in a wide range of specialized courses, in 'Modern Britain' and 'Comparative Sociology' courses, and in integrated introductory courses. They have been written with the newcomer and general reader in mind, and they meet the genuine need in the informed public for accurate and up-to-date discussion and sources.

John Scott
Series Editor

Acknowledgements

Thanks and gratitude are due to all the colleagues and researchers whose findings and arguments are used in this book, even though some will have reservations about my uses. I would like to express special thanks to Sally Dench, Rebecca Hutten, and Paul Mooney for their assistance; they know why. Also, and certainly not least, I thank Clare Minghella who word processed the successive versions of the manuscript.

University of Liverpool   K.R.

Contents

List of Figures

List of Tables

Chapter One

Youth's New Condition

LEAVING SCHOOL IN THE MID-1970S

In 1976 West and Newton studied 174 leavers from two Nottinghamshire schools.

32 per cent obtained the first jobs that they applied for.

86 per cent had jobs within a month of leaving school.

M. West and P. Newton, *The Transition from School to Work* (Croom Helm, London, 1983).

West and Newton's study was one of the last British inquiries to be completed before school-leavers' prospects changed radically. In their research West and Newton paid a great deal of attention to the careers advice and the other types of vocational preparation that the young people received in their secondary schools. They paid little attention to youth unemployment. In the early 1970s this was a problem only in Britain's depressed regions and among specific 'problem groups' such as persistent truants, young offenders, and other young people who seemed unable to settle and hold onto any jobs (Baxter 1975). Further education in their schools or local colleges did not feature in the plans of many of the young people in West and Newton's study. Unless 16-year-olds were taking GCE O-levels and were expecting to perform well it was taken for granted that they would leave school and start work at the earliest opportunity. Most secondary schools had no sixth form places except for students who took the two or three A-levels that were needed to enter higher education. Training schemes did not feature in West and Newton's study because until 1976 there were none except 'Community Industry', which had been introduced in 1972 to cater specifically for those young people who were incapable of obtaining or, more typically, of holding on to the jobs that were then plentiful in most parts of Britain (Shanks 1982).

The youth employment scene and, indeed, the entire process through which young people enter the work-force in Britain, is very different in the 1990s. Yet the focus of interest for many sociologists remains virtually unchanged. When studying young people and their employment, sociologists have always typically addressed two central and seemingly perennial questions: occupational placement and occupational socialization.

Perennial question 1: occupational placement

The first perennial topic of interest concerns matters of *occupational role allocation* and *social placement* more generally. Sociologists want to know *who* gets which jobs, *how*, and *why*. The types of jobs that individuals enter during the early stages in their working careers are the best predictors of the types of employment that they will hold for the rest of their lives. Hence the importance of the occupational role allocation that occurs when young people first enter the labour market.

Jobs are arranged in a hierarchy of desirability. They differ considerably in terms of pay, status, opportunities for career progression, and job satisfaction, and these rewards are not arranged in compensatory patterns. In general the most satisfying jobs are not the worst paid: quite the reverse. And jobs are important not only from the point of view of individuals' quality of working life. Their types of employment govern individuals' broader *life chances*; the types of houses and districts where they are able to live, and the kinds of leisure that they are able to enjoy and make available to their children. People's jobs locate them not only in the economy but also in the broader *social class structure*.

The entry into employment is not the only stage that matters in the lifetime class and status attainment process. Individuals' life chances may be influenced by their genetic make-up as determined at conception. Children's experiences in their families of origin certainly shape the abilities and aspirations that they acquire. These, along with their genetic make-up, affect their performances in education, which then becomes the best single predictor of their future employment prospects.

By the time that they leave school, young people have built up stocks of different types and amounts of capital. Some have *economic* capital—savings and investments usually made on their behalf, or prospects of inheritance from other family members. However, there are equally important *social* and *cultural* types of capital. These consist of social relationships (contacts and connections with influential people), qualifications, attitudes and values, behaviour and speech patterns. All these assets can influence individuals' prospects when they enter the labour market. But young people usually need to convert their capital, whatever this might be, into specific occupational attainments in order to obtain the best possible returns during their adult lives. Educational qualifications are the most useful of all the non-economic types of capital in this conversion process, but in market economies these qualifications have never conferred an automatic right to a commensurate job. Qualifications improve individuals' chances, but they are not automatically converted into employment. Some young people fail to obtain the types of employment to which their capital might have been expected to lead. They may be poor interviewees or easily discouraged when their job applications are unsuccessful. Others succeed despite their lack of assets. Success and failure during the early stages of working life are important because initial jobs then take over from educational qualifications as the best predictors of individuals' future labour market prospects.

Needless to say, the jobs that they enter early in their working lives do not rigidly determine individuals' futures. Many of the young people in the 1960s and 70s who believed that the skills acquired in their apprenticeships would last them for life, have been proved to have been over-optimistic (Ryrie and Weir 1978). In the past some people's careers recovered after unpromising starts. Some, though not all, of those who started out on the lower rungs of professional and management careers in the 1950s and 60s eventually reached the summits of the bureaucratic hierarchies that dominate the public and private sectors. Other adults have experienced social demotion when their jobs, firms, and entire industries in some cases disappeared, thereby devaluing all their occupational skills, knowledge, and experience. In the 1990s the future appears—and probably really is—even more difficult to predict than in previous decades. Even so, the step from education into employment has been and is still one of the most critical stages in the lifetime attainment process. It is impossible to be certain about the future but everything that we know about our present-day society suggests that these steps remain as important in the 1990s as in earlier years. Hence the importance of continuing to ask which young people enter which jobs, how, and why. Sociologists are particularly interested in how life chances are distributed according to individuals' social backgrounds as defined by their family origins, gender, ethnic groups, and places of residence. Have these predictors become more or less influential and divisive than in the past?

Perennial question 2: occupational socialization

A second set of questions that lead sociologists to investigate transitions into employment concern *vocational preparation, occupational socialization,* or the *socio-cultural and technical reproduction of the work-force*. Which of these phrases is used is basically a matter of theoretical preference, but the basic problem is always how turnover of labour force personnel occurs while the work-force's skills and vocationally relevant attitudes, and the social relationships within which people work, remain intact. Given that human beings have finite lifetimes, how is it possible for social patterns to persist over time? Obviously enough, these patterns must be transmitted down the generations. How does this happen in economic life? If the transmission does not occur, what are the impediments and the consequences for the individuals who cannot be fitted into the economy, and for the wider society?

These questions are really incredibly complicated. Whatever the area of social life, processes of reproduction are always problematic: they may not occur, and if they do this can be by various means. Functionalist and Marxist theories (for example Bowles and Gintis 1976) have often exaggerated the correspondences between what children learn through their experiences in their homes and schools, and what is expected of them in adult life. These theories have tacitly or explicitly assumed that social systems more or less automatically bring about the correspondences that are needed if the systems are to persist over time. In practice young people may fail to learn skills that the economy requires, though it is very difficult to establish exactly what any economy really needs. We cannot simply assume that previous workers' skills and attitudes were the best of all possibilities.

In Britain in recent years there has been much debate about the education system's alleged failure to teach the knowledge and skills that are required by a modern 'world class' economy. Employers regularly criticize school-leavers and even university-leavers for their deficiencies in basic abilities such as spelling and arithmetic. Young people's attitudes have also attracted criticism; particularly an alleged reluctance to respect authority and an unwillingness to apply themselves to training. But it could be a mistake to treat employers' accusations as if they were obviously and objectively true. It is by no means certain that employers necessarily even know which mixes of skills would give the best economic results.

Evidence of British school-leavers lagging behind other countries' young people in basic educational standards and vocational skills is often produced. Even if this evidence is accepted at face value it does not necessarily follow that other countries will have superior adult workers. The additional skills that they bring to the labour market could be surplus to economic requirements. Alternatively, British workers may catch up rapidly once in employment. Even if the economies of all the countries with allegedly superior education were out-performing Britain, it would still not be absolutely safe to assume that differences in labour supply were the explanation: superior education could be a consequence, rather than a cause, of economic success.

Discrepancies between the skills that new workers can offer and those that employers expect are always likely to arise in changing societies, where the fundamental need is not to reproduce unchanging work-forces but to keep existing and future employees abreast or ahead of changing requirements. New technology, changes in consumer demand, and in a society's position in the international economy may result in rapid shifts in labour demand. School and university syllabuses in education are frequently criticized for being out of date and for failing to meet the standards of businesses that are at the leading edge. Employers and politicians frequently argue that British businesses receive less assistance from education in these respects than do their overseas competitors. Yet, once again, the fact that this criticism is frequently made does not make it true. Industry may be able to tolerate an imperfect match between what new workers can offer and job requirements. Training after entry and informal workplace socialization may bridge any gaps. Indeed, these may be the best ways of synchronizing labour demand and supply under rapidly changing economic conditions. A degree of disorder between job requirements and beginners' capacities may even be helpful as it can allow businesses to shape new young workers in accordance with their specific needs. The following chapters repeatedly consider, but are consistently sceptical towards, claims that British firms are obliged to adopt low skill, low cost, low wage strategies on account of the quality of labour supply. Would Britain really leap into the division of high tech, high skilled, high wage economies if only vocational preparation were overhauled?

Mismatches between the supply and demand for youth labour may be due to the absence of opportunities in education and training which would allow young people to meet employers' requirements. Alternatively, they may result from a failure of young people to use the education and training that is available, or to apply themselves when on the courses. Young people may fail to grasp opportunities through ignorance of their existence or of the career rewards that would eventually follow, in which case better careers information and guidance might be a remedy. Industrialists sometimes complain that too many school- and college-leavers have either taken the wrong courses or lack enthusiasm due to their ignorance of careers in manufacturing. Another possibility, however, is that young people may not wish to equip themselves for some of the jobs that they see lying ahead. They may be unattracted by the rewards and may therefore resist their apparent futures.

During the last twenty years, much has been written about the various ways in which working-class young people endeavour to resist the demands of all adult authorities. Working-class youth cultures have been interpreted as forms of resistance. In 1977, in his influential book *Learning to Labour*, Paul Willis drew attention to a paradox. In resisting authority in and out of school, young working-class males were in fact becoming well prepared for the working-class occupational cultures that they were mostly destined to enter. This argument is discussed in more detail in Chapter Four. For present purposes it is sufficient to note that resistance may, but will not necessarily and automatically, be transformed into accommodation, and, in any case, an analysis that applied in the 1970s may not hold in the 1990s. In recent years a debate has arisen about the creation of a new underclass whose members, it is alleged, have little interest in taking or holding onto the types of employment for which they either are, or could become, qualified. It has been argued, for example, that some prefer lifestyles based on crime and state benefits. However, even if such an underclass is being created, it will not necessarily follow that the economy will be the victim. The culture could have spread because the economy has neither need nor use for all young people's labour.

The changing national context

By now it will be clear why perennial questions about who gets which jobs and occupational socialization need to be addressed afresh by successive generations. Change is a ubiquitous feature of modern life. Each generation seems to see itself as experiencing momentous social changes, but it is undoubtedly the case that the situations of young people have been overhauled thoroughly during the last twenty years, arguably more thoroughly than at any time since the introduction of compulsory schooling. Hence the high profile debate in recent years on 'youth's new social condition'.

There has been a dramatic decline in youth employment, most particularly in full-time youth employment. At the time when the statutory school-leaving age was last raised (from 15 to 16 in 1972) nearly two-thirds of all young people were leaving school at the earliest opportunity and all but a small minority obtained jobs more or less immediately. By the early 1990s less than one in ten 16-year-olds were leaving school and entering employment. Britain's young workers of the 1970s have been replaced by the students, trainees, and young unemployed of the 1990s. Far fewer teenagers are now wage or salary earning. More are claiming state benefits of various types but the main growth has been in young people's dependence on their families.

Table 1 Activity Status at age 16–17

Year	Cohort	FT Education	FT Job	Scheme	Un-employed	Other	Weighted Base (n)
1985	1*	37	29	17	15	2	8064
1986	2*	38	22	28	10	1	14430
1987	3	43	23	26	8	1	16208
1989	4	50	24	22	3	2	14116
1991	5	58	18	14	7	2	14511
1992	6	66	13	11	7	2	24922

* State Maintained Schools only.
Source: England and Wales Youth Cohort Surveys (see page 24).

Table 1 presents some basic information from the England and Wales Youth Cohort Surveys, a series of inquiries which began in 1985 and which have followed up successive cohorts of 16-year-olds. In spring 1985 a representative sample of young people who became eligible to leave school during the previous summer was surveyed, and similar surveys have been conducted in later years. In 1985 only 29 per cent of 16–17-year-olds had full-time jobs and by 1992 this proportion had dropped to 13 per cent. Youth Training accommodated many of the young people who were unable to obtain jobs in the late-1980s, over a quarter of 16–17-year-olds in 1986 and 1987, but the proportion of young people entering this scheme then declined to 11 per cent in 1992. The big growth was in the numbers staying in full-time education. These almost doubled from 37 per cent in 1985 to 66 per cent in 1992. Since 1986 less than 10 per cent of 16–17-year-olds have been unemployed but this figure understates the extent to which school-leavers have been frustrated when seeking jobs. Throughout the period covered in Table 1 the numbers unemployed and on Youth Training exceeded the numbers of 16-17-year-olds in employment.

SCHOOLS COUNCIL INQUIRY, 1, *YOUNG SCHOOL-LEAVERS* (HMSO, London, 1968)

In 1968, when 15 was the statutory school-leaving age, the Schools Council, a government advisory body at the time, published the results of a survey among 4,825 13–16-year-old secondary school pupils and their parents.

Three-quarters of the pupils thought that being at work would definitely be better than being at school.

Half of the boys and two-thirds of the girls were planning to leave school at 15 and had no intention of pursuing any further education.

Two-thirds of the parents believed that 15 was the right age for their children to leave school.

Half of the parents were unreservedly opposed to raising the school-leaving age.

The changes in young people's situations of the last twenty years have not been in response to pressure from or at the request of young people. If young people's own wishes had been decisive the majority would still be leaving school and entering employment at age 15 and they would be doing so with the support of their parents. Young people have not been the initiators but they have been affected profoundly by broader economic and educational changes.

Before turning to the effects of the changes of the last twenty years on young people's occupational role allocation and socialization, it will be helpful to sketch an overview of the changes themselves.

The decline of youth employment

The principal change has undoubtedly been the decline in youth employment itself. Unemployment levels throughout the UK work-force have been much higher since the 1970s than in the 1950s and 60s. The recessions of the 1980s and 90s have been deeper than those experienced during the so-called thirty glorious years of almost continuous economic growth and full employment that lasted from 1945 up to the early 1970s. Subsequently there have been insufficient jobs to accommodate all would-be workers, and teenagers' difficulties have been one aspect of this wider unemployment problem. However, employment among young people has declined much more sharply than the pace at which general unemployment has risen, and youth employment failed to recover during the economic boom in the mid-to-late 1980s.

Two explanations have been offered for young workers' exceptional vulnerability. As is often the case with apparently competing theories, both make valid points and need not be treated as incompatible alternatives. One theory, associated with Peter Makeham and David Raffe, argues that in Britain young people have normally been especially sensitive to any general trends in employment and unemployment. In times of rising unemployment young people have been particularly vulnerable for three reasons. First, employers slow down recruitment and this always has especially strong effects among newcomers to the labour market who have no existing jobs to hang on to. Secondly, when profit margins have been under pressure, British employers have often made savings on training. Firms have been reluctant to train young people when they have felt unable to guarantee future employment. Employers have often taken the view that such training would waste the young people's time as well as the firms' resources. Thirdly, in times of high unemployment school-leavers have needed to compete for jobs against displaced adults whose experience has often given them the edge. Makeham (1980) and Raffe (1985) have argued that it is unnecessary to look beyond these factors to account for the spread of youth unemployment in the 1970s and early 1980s.

In contrast, David Ashton and his colleagues (Ashton and Maguire 1983; Ashton et al. 1989) have argued that young people have simultaneously been victims of economic and occupational restructuring. Alongside the rise in levels of unemployment there have been major changes in the structure of the UK economy and, therefore, in the types of employment that are available. Employment in manufacturing industries has declined steeply whereas there are now more jobs in services. White-collar employment has increased as a proportion of all jobs, while manual employment—especially manual work in manufacturing—has declined. Part-time jobs, especially in service sectors such as retailing, hotels, and restaurants, have been a growing proportion of all jobs. Rates of labour market participation by adult women have risen and they now occupy a higher proportion of all jobs than in the 1970s, and a particularly high proportion of part-time jobs. Amidst all these changes David Ashton and his colleagues have argued that young people's job chances have proved highly vulnerable. Young males have been greatly affected by the decline of employment in manufacturing, which has led to the disappearance of most of the craft apprenticeships and less skilled occupations that they once entered. Female school-leavers have also been affected by these changes, but to a lesser extent. However, they have been vulnerable in the face of labour market competition from older females and the restructuring of many of their former full-time jobs into part-time occupations.

Ashton's explanation of the decline in youth employment in terms of restructuring gains support from the failure of youth employment to recover during the economic boom of the 1980s. The UK economy expanded from 1982 until the onset of the recession in the early 1990s and general unemployment fell from 1986 onwards, but there was no rise in the numbers of 16- and 17-year-olds in full-time jobs. Growth was failing to recreate youth jobs partly because most of the employment growth was in business sectors and occupations where there was no tradition of employing this age group. In addition, by the mid-1980s most employers and young people seemed to have adjusted to and thereby normalized the exclusion of 16- and 17-year-olds from full-time employment. By then, most 16-year-olds were staying in full-time education or entering Youth Training, and employers were targeting scheme-leavers or school- and college-leavers aged 18 and above when recruiting beginners (Roberts *et al.* 1987).

The withdrawal of their former job opportunities has been just one side of the changes that have created new social conditions for youth. The other part of the story has been the creation of new places for the young in education and training. Many young people, and their parents, have rejected these new opportunities as poor substitutes for jobs. Their best verdict on the new education and training schemes has been that these opportunities are, on balance, preferable to unemployment. Some researchers, including the present author, have argued that a major function of some of the new courses and training schemes has been to 'warehouse' young people until jobs become available and, in the meantime, both to reduce the unemployment figures and prevent the young people's skills and motivation deteriorating. When 'special measures' were first introduced for unemployed teenagers in the 1970s, the government viewed them in more or less these terms. The official report that led to the introduction of the Youth Opportunities Programme in 1978 argued that, 'We must not lose sight of the fact that the ideal situation is one in which a young person gets a satisfactory job and does not enter the programme at all. If that aim is to be pursued, possible interference with the normal working of the labour market must be minimised . . . To make an opportunity available for every unemployed young person would be absurd and undesirable even if it were feasible, which, in our view, it is not' (Manpower Services Commission 1977: 43). When the Youth Opportunities Programme was launched young people had to serve a qualifying period of six weeks' unemployment before they could enter, and they were expected to remain available for employment (and seeking work) throughout their time on the Programme. In the 1970s, all the government measures to create alternatives for unemployed young people were described as 'special' or 'temporary'. At that time the measures were not meant to become permanent fixtures.

Nevertheless, a constant body of opinion has argued that the decline of youth employment should not be regarded as a problem but as an opportunity. If young people are no longer required as producers then, it has been argued, we should seize the opportunity to invest in their education and training. Britain, it has been claimed, has been handicapped by a less educated, less trained, and less skilled work-force than its main economic competitors. The previous section of this chapter invited scepticism towards such claims but, whatever their validity, these views have influenced government responses to the decline of youth employment since the early 1980s. The Youth Training Scheme which replaced the Youth Opportunities Programme in 1983 was not intended to be another temporary measure. In 1983 the government stressed that this new scheme should be regarded as a training measure first and foremost, rather than a response to youth unemployment, and intended the scheme to become a permanent bridge between school and work for 16- and 17-year-old school-leavers. Since 1983 the government view has been that young people's new opportunities will help to achieve a closer match between the economy's needs and what beginning workers can offer. In other words, occupational socialization is supposed to have been improved. At the same time, it was claimed when the new opportunities were introduced that they would be especially beneficial for young people who were formerly the least advantaged in the labour market—poorly qualified secondary school-leavers, females, and ethnic minorities for example (Manpower Services Commission 1981*a* and 1981*b*). By opening new routes into employment the new provisions were supposed to make a difference to who gets which jobs. Whether the measures have in fact made any difference in these respects is considered in detail in Chapter Three.

The new vocationalism in education

One set of new opportunities has been created by a government-led revival of vocational education. The origins of the new vocationalism are usually traced to a speech delivered by James Callaghan, then Prime Minister, at Ruskin College in 1976 in which he accused the schools of perhaps paying too much attention to developing each individual's potential at the expense of teaching them how to earn their livings. This speech was followed by a Great Debate, led by the Secretary of State for Education, Shirley Williams, in which the main events were regional conferences to which leading industrialists and representatives of education were invited.

One immediate product of this debate was a spread of work experience programmes in secondary schools. Work experience spread rapidly and by the end of the 1980s it had become a standard feature in the syllabuses of most secondary schools. By 1988–9 91 per cent of secondary schools were arranging work experience and 71 per cent of all pupils were involved (National Curriculum Council, 1991).

However, in the late 1970s the government pinned more hopes on another initiative. 'It is the government's intention to establish during the 1980s a universal scheme of education and training opportunities for young people' (Department of Education and Science 1979: 1). This universal scheme was to be *Unified Vocational Preparation*, six-month programmes aimed primarily at the young people who were leaving school and entering employment in which they received no systematic training or continuing education. While this policy was being formulated the jobs that the government hoped to enrich were disappearing for good.

The new vocationalism in education really gathered momentum in the early 1980s. In 1983 a Technical and Vocational Education Initiative (TVEI) was announced. This initiative began with pilot schemes and was subsequently made available to all secondary schools. As was the case with many initiatives in education during the 1980s, TVEI was administered by the Employment Department through the Manpower Services Commission. This initiative made funds available for schools to enrich their technical and vocational education, usually by acquiring micro-computers, but also, it was intended, by giving a vocational slant to the entire curriculum—science, geography, history, and languages as well as technical subjects themselves.

During the 1980s a growing proportion of government funds for further education were channelled through the Manpower Services Commission rather than from the Department of Education and

Science via Local Education Authorities. The aim was to make further education more responsive to industry's needs. However, the introduction of National Vocational Qualifications (NVQs) was the main means whereby the government tried to strengthen and upgrade vocational studies in post-compulsory education. The National Council for Vocational Qualifications that was created in 1986 does not itself run courses or even award most NVQs. Rather it has created a framework composed of five levels within which other organizations' qualifications can be located. The purpose of this framework has been to systematize 'the jungle' of vocational qualifications, and to enhance their visibility and appeal. Many NVQs are designed for persons in employment or employer-led training, but others can be gained through full-time education. NVQs recognize skills required in particular occupations and industries whereas General NVQs (GNVQs) recognize broader-based pre-career vocational preparation. In the early 1990s the government announced targets in terms of the proportions of young people who, it hoped, would be gaining NVQs or GNVQs at different levels by 1995. The government wanted all 18-year-olds to have had the opportunity to achieve at least Level 2 (roughly equivalent to a good set of GCSE passes) and 50 per cent to be achieving Level 3 or the alleged academic equivalent of two A-levels.

Youth Training

The second strand in the government's efforts to improve vocational preparation in the 1980s was the development of youth training. Here the main initiative was the Youth Training Scheme (YTS) which replaced the Youth Opportunities Programme (YOP) in 1983. YOP had normally offered just six months' work experience whereas YTS was introduced as 'quality training' leading to 'recognized qualifications' and normally lasting for a year at first but for up to two years from 1986 onwards. Most training places were employer-based but had to include the equivalent of a day per week off-the-job training. Very quickly YTS became the normal next step for 16-year-old school-leavers in many parts of Britain. One-step transitions, straight from compulsory education into employment, were replaced by two-step transitions via youth training or post-compulsory education.

How YTS operated and its short-term and long-term impacts on the processes of entering the work-force are examined in detail in Chapter Three. However, from 1988 onwards the administration of YTS was handed to the newly created Training and Enterprise Councils (TECs) in England and Wales and LECs (Local Enterprise Councils) in

Scotland. These councils were composed mainly of employers appointed by the Secretary of State for Employment, and were intended to tailor YTS and other Employment Department measures to the needs of local economies. Under the auspices of the TECs and LECs YTS became a more flexible and varied scheme. In 1990 the scheme became known simply as Youth Training, and from 1991 onwards it began to be replaced by Youth Credits or Training Credits—entitlements distributed through the TECs and LECs which enabled young people to 'purchase' approved forms of training up to a specified value.

By then Youth Training was contracting, partly on account of the demographic trend, the declining size of school-leaving cohorts (see below), but also because this initiative was losing ground to its competitors. The different ways in which the government was promoting vocational preparation were partly in competition with one another. Colleges offering full-time courses leading to vocational qualifications and training schemes run by employers and other trainers were in direct competition with each other, and with the other opportunities (jobs in some cases and, more significantly, academic courses) that young people were being offered. In 1994 the government announced the creation of Modern Apprenticeships, employer-based training leading to Level 3 NVQs, in an attempt to strengthen the training route to skills and into the work-force.

Deregulating the youth labour market

Recent governments have not been single-minded when addressing school-to-work transition problems. They have supported portfolios of policies and measures, and the 'multi-club' approach is certainly not a post-1970s novelty. It has always been recognized that different groups of young people require different types of provisions. The same recipe—academic education or employer-based training for example—would not get the same response or have the same effects throughout the age group. However, different measures have sometimes reflected differences in political philosophy some of which have divided, while others have coexisted within, Britain's main parties. The various views of political influentials, who include youth researchers, have added to the heterogeneity in policies and provisions.

It should not be a source of surprise, therefore, that the same government that was promoting vocational education and training in the 1980s was simultaneously trying to revive youth employment. The only historical shock was that from the nineteenth century up to the 1970s there had been a broad consensus among politicians of all parties that children and young people needed special protection from the operation of raw labour market forces whereas by the 1980s a politically ascendant body of opinion was urging deregulation, meaning that restrictions on hours and conditions of work and rates of pay should be removed because the burden that these restrictions placed on employers was job destructive. This remedy for unemployment was considered especially appropriate for young people.

It was argued in the early 1980s, and accepted by the government, that there was a strong case for encouraging youth rates of pay to float downwards to levels at which the labour market would clear. Young people, it was claimed, were being priced out of employment. It was said that they had become more expensive during the decades of full employment when trade unions had been able to negotiate attractive pay for apprentices and other beginners. The raising of the school-leaving age in the early 1970s, fast on the heels of a lowering of the previously recognized age of majority, 21, was said to have made young people significantly more expensive to employ, and their wage rates were said to be making them unemployable in a period when general levels of unemployment gave employers scope for choice (Wells 1983).

Between 1982 and 1988 the Young Workers Scheme and the New Workers Scheme offered subsidies to employers who hired young people provided the rates of pay were significantly beneath the average for the age group. There were no stipulations as regards the training that the young people should receive; employers received the subsidy irrespective of the type of work or training if the young workers were sufficiently low paid. In 1986 young people were removed from the protection of the Wages Councils, which set minimum rates of pay in industries where trade unions and collective bargaining were weak. In 1993 these Councils were abolished completely. It seemed that deregulation was being piloted on young people before being applied to other age groups. In 1989 some of the protective legislation which restricted young people's (and women's) hours and conditions of work and the occupations in which they could be employed was repealed. Also, in 1988 most unemployed 16- and 17-year-olds lost their entitlement to social security. This change was presented as removing the 'option' of youth unemployment and was among a larger set of measures intended to erode a dependency or claimant culture which was said to be inflating the costs of social security and creating a permanently out-of-work hardcore. The inset on page 16 summarizes the main changes that were made between 1980 and 1993 towards reducing young people's dependence on state welfare. The benefit entitlements of unemployed young people were progressively reduced. Those in employment lost some of their former protection. Students in further and higher education were made more dependent on loans and their families.

WITHDRAWAL OF STATE WELFARE

1980	3 months waiting period for school-leavers.
	Exclusion of further education students from benefits (21-hour rule).
	Exceptional needs payments (eg. to set up a home) curtailed.
1983	16–17-year-olds living at home lose contribution towards board.
1984	Extended to 18–20-year-olds.
1986	Young people's wages removed from Wages Council regulation.
1986	21–4-year-olds living at home lose contribution towards board. Those living away receive board for only 4–6 weeks.
1987	Students: no supplementary benefit during short vacation.
1988	Supplementary benefit withdrawn from most 16- and 17-year-olds.
	Adult rate of benefit only from age 26, unless parents.
1989	Repeal of employment protection legislation.
1990	Students lose housing benefit.
	Student loans introduced, grant 'frozen'.
1991	No income support for students during long vacation.
1993	Student grant reduced.

A parallel set of measures aimed to make young people more enterprising. Schools were encouraged to teach enterprise values and for a time enterprise became a required part of the curricula on all Youth Training Schemes. From age 18 young people could be assisted out of unemployment by an Enterprise Allowance which offered £40 per week for a year to unemployed individuals with plans for embarking into self-employment which satisfied the scheme organizers, provided they could show that they were able to invest at least £1,000 of their own or someone else's capital.

None of the measures intended to revive youth employment were clearly successful in straightforward quantitative terms. The government subsidies to low paid youth jobs were mostly 'deadweight', that is, paid to employers who would have recruited young people even in the absence of the subsidies (Bushell 1986; Rajan 1985). Economists were never agreed that pay was a significant barrier to youth employment (see Junakar 1987). Large companies did not reduce their youth wage rates to take advantage of the subsidies. They pointed out that youth wages were a tiny proportion of their total costs and that they had no intention of jeopardizing their industrial relations or destabilizing their existing pay structures merely because the government had introduced yet another scheme which, in any case, was likely to be temporary (Roberts *et al.* 1987). Young people who tried to work on their own accounts were more often motivated by an ethic of survival than a spirit of enterprise. They were typically forced into self-employment because of their inability to obtain proper jobs (see MacDonald and Coffield 1991). However, the gap between youth and adult rates of pay did widen in the 1980s (*Bargaining Report* 1986). Labour market conditions were the main force holding down youth wages but the state measures that were introduced—subsidies for low paid jobs plus the levels at which the allowances paid to youth trainees were set, and the erosion of young people's social security entitlements—would have reinforced market mechanisms. Deregulation may have prevented youth unemployment rising even higher and youth employment declining to an even greater extent. From young people's points of view, however, this was probably a mixed blessing. They retained the option of looking for jobs from age 16 but many of the jobs that were available were 'poor jobs'—low paid and in marginal businesses that were unable to offer security or attractive working conditions. The type of dead-end juvenile jobs that had existed before the Second World War, but which had been driven off the labour market in the subsequent conditions of full employment, began to be recreated in the 1980s.

Academic courses and qualifications

In so far as there was competition for young people it was clear by the early 1990s that education was beating both the market in proper jobs and Youth Training, and within education the longer established academic courses and qualifications were retaining their appeal against the new vocational challengers. This was not completely contrary to the government's intentions because its policies included strengthening academic education. While it was encouraging schools to make their teaching vocationally relevant, the government was also advocating a strengthening of traditional basic standards.

The 1988 Education Reform Act was the centre-piece in the

government's measures towards educational reform in the 1980s. This Act introduced a national curriculum for all 5- to 16-year-olds in state schools which bore a close resemblance to traditional grammar school education and made few concessions to vocationalism. National testing of pupils was authorized by the Act. The government's intention was to publish 'league tables' while widening parental choice of schools and gearing schools' budgets to the numbers of pupils that were enrolled. Subsequently similar market disciplines were introduced into further and higher education. Schools and colleges competed for students and during the 1980s enrolments in each sector increased. The proportion of England's 17-year-olds in schools rose from 17.7 to 28 per cent between 1979–80 and 1991–2 while the proportion in further education rose from 9.1 per cent to 20.7 per cent (see Table 2).

Table 2 England: 17-year-olds; Percentages of age group in various educational institutions

	1979–80	1985–6	1991–2
Higher Education	0.3	0.2	0.3
Schools	17.7	18.9	28.0
Further Education	9.1	12.9	20.7
Total	27.1	32.0	49.0

In 1988 the General Certificate of Education Ordinary Level and the Certificate of Secondary Education were merged into a single General Certificate of Secondary Education (GCSE), and as soon as this new examination came into operation in 1988 the proportion of pupils gaining higher grade passes increased thus continuing a longer-term trend (see Table 3). The stay-on rate beyond age 16 rose to around 50 per cent in the late 1980s and to over 70 per cent in the early 1990s. The numbers taking A-levels also rose, and likewise the numbers proceeding into higher education. By the early 1990s the student population in higher education was equivalent to a third of the 18–21 age group that had traditionally provided the majority of students. This expansion occurred at a time when the government was transferring more of the costs of higher education onto students and their families. Table 4 describes what happened to student grants from 1979 onwards. Students' eligibility for most social security and housing benefits was withdrawn, while in the early 1990s grants were frozen, then reduced, and supplemented by loans. Despite the fears that these changes would restrict

Table 3 GCSE/GCE/CSE/SCE attainments of young people as a percentage of the relevant population[1]

	1970/1	1975/6	1980/1	1985/6	1989/90	1990/1
1 or more GCE A-levels or SCE H-grades[2]						
All students[3]	......	19	20	22	26	28
School-leavers only	16.6	16.9	17.0	17.8	21.8	23.2
No A-levels or SCE H-grades (school leavers)[4]						
5 or more higher grades[5]	7.1	8.2	8.9	10.5	11.3	11.7
1–4 higher grades[5]	16.8	23.9	24.8	26.7	26.2	24.8
1 or more other grades[6]	9.8	27.8	30.6	32.7	25.4	24.1
No graded results	44.0	18.7	13.5	11.7	8.3	7.5

[1] Based on population aged 17 years at 31 August preceding the academic year for five or more higher GCSE/GCE O-level/CSE grades and above, and aged 15 years for other qualification levels.
[2] Includes students with two AS levels.
[3] School pupils and young home students at tertiary and other further education establishments, estimated and rounded to the nearest percentage point.
[4] Includes students with one AS level.
[5] Grades A–C at GCSE/GCE O-level and grade 1 at CSE. Includes Scottish O/S grades 1–3/A–C.
[6] Grades D–G at GCSE, grades D, E at GCE O-level (except 1970/1, when no such award was made) and grades 2–5 at CSE. Includes Scottish O/S grades 4–5/D–E.

access especially among social groups traditionally under-represented in the universities, recruitment rose from all sections of the population.

However, access to higher education did not expand to quite the extent that some government announcements suggested. It was not the case in the early 1990s that a third of 18–20-year-olds were entering higher education. In 1991–2 the higher education participation rate among 19–20-year-olds was around one in five. Roughly a third of this age group was in some form of full-time or part-time education but only three-fifths of these were higher education students. The numbers in universities had risen to the equivalent of a third of this age group through the recruitment of more mature students, a trend which is discussed in Chapter Five.

Change and continuity

By the beginning of the 1990s the situations of young people had changed dramatically. Far fewer were in employment than in the mid-1970s. More were in academic and vocational education, and others

Table 4 Student awards: real value and parental contributions, England and Wales

Index of the real value of the grant deflated by

	Standard maintenance grant[1] (£)	Retail prices index[2]	Average earnings index[3]	Average assessed contribution by parents[4] (percentages)
1979/80	1,245	100	100	13
1980/1	1,430	97	99	13
1981/2	1,535	96	95	14
1982/3	1,595	93	91	19
1983/4	1,660	90	89	20
1984/5	1,775	89	89	25
1985/6	1,830	91	87	30
1986/7	1,901	88	82	30
1987/8	1,972	89	78	31
1988/9	2,050	87	74	31
1989/90	2,155	85	72	31
1990/1	2,265	81		

[1] Excludes those studying in London and those studying elsewhere living in the parental home. Prior to 1982/3 Oxford and Cambridge were also excluded. Since 1984/5 has included an additional travel allowance of £50.
[2] September 1979 = 100.
[3] Great Britain average earnings for the whole economy has been used as the deflator. February 1980 = 100.
[4] Assuming full payment of parental and other contributions including a notional assessment in respect of students for whom fees only were paid by LEAs. Of the students assessed for parental contributions in 1989/90 there were 107.4 thousand mandatory award holders (27 per cent) who were receiving the maximum grant because their parents' assessed contribution was nil.

Source: Department of Education and Science; Employment Department

were receiving Youth Training. Old routes through academic education had expanded, and new routes into employment via vocational education and training had been created. But exactly how much had been overhauled? Had the changes redistributed job opportunities between social groups—males and females, from different kinds of home backgrounds, and with different levels of attainment in their secondary schools? Had there been any changes in the fit, or the alleged lack of fit, between the economy's needs and what young people could offer? These questions are taken up in Chapters Three and Four.

Demography

Demography is the study of population. In the late 1980s in Britain there was much talk of an impending demographic time bomb. The birth-rate had declined from the 1960s through the 1970s. The result was fewer individuals reaching age 16, 18, then 21 in each year from 1983 onwards. Past birth-rates guaranteed that this trend would continue into the early 1990s. Britain in the late 1980s, or at least certain sections of its population, was celebrating continuous economic growth since 1982. Since 1986 unemployment had been falling. The explosion of the demographic time bomb was predicted in the early 1990s when economic growth and the demand for labour, especially skilled labour, were forecast to outstrip the supply, especially of well-qualified and trained labour. It was argued that employers would need to turn to non-traditional sources of skilled labour—women, ethnic minorities, unskilled adults, and young people with low or modest educational attainments (National Economic Development Office 1988).

The explosion never occurred. Britain's economy sank into recession in the early 1990s and this overwhelmed the demographic trend. Demography is not necessarily decisive in swinging labour market balances. The effects of given demographic trends always depend on other things remaining equal, or other trends continuing. However, demography is never entirely irrelevant, and from the mid-1990s onwards Britain's young people will be in a different demographic situation from their predecessors in the 1980s (see Figure I).

Throughout the 1980s the number of young people was declining. So one would have expected the *numbers* of unemployed young people,

Table 5 UK 19–20-year-old students as percentages of the age group

	Males		Females	
	1980–1	1991–2	1980–1	1991–2
Students	%	%	%	%
Full-time	13.8	20.6	11.0	20.3
Part-time	17.8	14.1	12.1	14.3
Total	31.6	34.8	23.1	34.6

Source: Department for Education, *Statistical Bulletin*, 1 (1994), London.

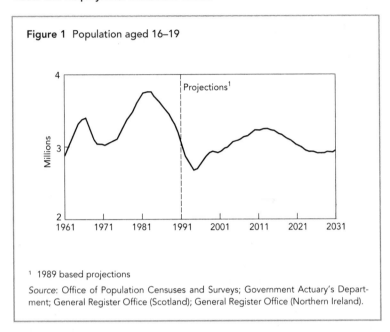

Figure 1 Population aged 16–19

¹ 1989 based projections

Source: Office of Population Censuses and Surveys; Government Actuary's Department; General Register Office (Scotland); General Register Office (Northern Ireland).

young offenders, and so on to decline even without any changes in the unemployment or crime *rates*. Education needed to hold on to a higher proportion of the over-16s if the system was not to contract in absolute terms, which would probably have meant widespread school closures and redundancies among teachers. In the late 1980s schools, colleges and training schemes were competing for diminishing numbers of young people. It was possible to accommodate higher proportions of 16-year-olds in schools and colleges, and to admit rising proportions of 18-year-olds to higher education, without providing all the extra resources that would have been necessary if the absolute numbers had risen as rapidly as the proportions.

Since 1992–3 the number of 16–18-year-olds has been rising and this new trend must continue throughout the 1990s and until 2010. These future demographics can be predicted more accurately and confidently than most other trends because the earlier birth-rate, which is already known, is the main determinant. This means that, compared with their predecessors in the 1980s, young people in the 1990s and early 2000s will face stiffer competition for jobs, training places, and places in higher education if all other things remain equal. The numbers being educated and trained may increase without any rise in the proportions. Once again, demography may not be decisive. Rapid economic growth or an expansion of higher education places, for example, could overwhelm the new demographic trend. But the effects of any economic downturn will be amplified by the new demographic situation.

Research

Youth and employment has been a major research field since the 1970s. Paradoxically, the scarcer young people's employment opportunities have become, the more attention has been paid to their preparation for and eventual entry into the labour market. There was far less research among youth in the labour market in the 1960s and 70s. At that time the basic facts of the situation were well known and, in any case, the transition into employment was not a high profile social problem. Youth researchers were more likely to investigate delinquency or youth cultures more generally.

This changed as soon as youth unemployment became a national issue during the 1970s. The facts were no longer known and agreed so investigators set about discovering exactly what was happening to different groups of school-leavers as overall levels of joblessness rose. Most research into youth and employment issues since the 1970s has been policy centred. Most inquiries have been guided by one or both of two sets of questions. The first has concerned the effects of broader economic and labour market changes among young people. Specifically, researchers have investigated which groups have been affected most adversely, the types of damage that they have suffered, and how they have coped. These inquiries have typically sought young people's own views about, and responses to, their situations in the labour market, and to their old and new opportunities in education and training. The second set of questions has concerned the needs and demands of employers. These have sometimes been investigated and sometimes inferred from other evidence prior to examining whether young people acquire the relevant skills and knowledge in their education and training.

There have been scores of separate inquiries by independent researchers in different parts of the country, and in addition there have been some major research programmes in response to 'the problem' of youth's new condition. One such programme is the England and Wales Youth Cohort Surveys (see page 24), and another was the Economic and Social Research Council (ESRC) 16–19 Initiative (see page 25).

ENGLAND AND WALES YOUTH COHORT SURVEYS

This series of inquiries began in 1985 with a survey of a nationally representative sample of young people who had been in their final compulsory year,
normally the fifth forms, in their secondary schools, in 1984. The 1984 cohort
was surveyed on two further occasions in 1986 and 1987. There have been
similar longitudinal studies of subsequent 16-year-old cohorts. The findings
from each sweep of each cohort are published in the Employment
Department's *Youth Cohort Series*.

The advantages of these inquiries are:

- The samples are nationally representative.

- The cohorts are studied longitudinally, which enables the development of
  individuals' careers to be tracked.

- Successive cohorts have been studied. These surveys are therefore our
  best source of information on recent trends in participation in post-compulsory education, Youth Training, and rates of employment and unemployment among young people. The overview of recent trends in earlier
  sections of this chapter was based partly on the findings from the Youth
  Cohort surveys.

Scotland has a similar series of inquiries, The Scottish Young People's Survey
(see page 71).

Northern Ireland also has its own, albeit less regular, cohort studies.

The international context

A noteworthy trend since the 1970s is that research has become
increasingly internationally aware and co-ordinated. This is partly
because researchers and policy makers in most European countries
have realized that their young people have been affected by very similar trends. Hence the motivation to share experiences. However, the
internationalization of youth and employment research has also been
a response to the broader internationalization of economic life. This
has led to a realization in the UK, and in other countries, that, for example, young people's vocational preparation has to be judged against
European and world standards rather than just the customary expectations of domestic employers.

Hitherto sociology has normally studied the social systems of different countries. This book is conventional in this respect, but one school
of thought sees this form of sociology as becoming outdated by the

increasing significance of transnational processes. Manufactured products and financial services are marketed internationally, often by multinational corporations which operate in many countries and sometimes across several continents. Films, music, television programmes and other cultural products also now circulate globally. Students have become more likely to study in foreign countries. Britain is among Europe's more backward countries in this respect. There is also more international mobility of labour; not just the type of permanent migration that has occurred throughout history but also today in careers that straddle many countries.

Maybe it is premature to predict the death of nation states. Countries look certain to remain meaningful entities beyond this book's shelf life. Yet it is undeniable that countries have become more interdependent in international political and economic systems. Britain's economic well-being increasingly depends on its businesses' ability to hold their own against foreign-based competitors even within the UK market.

THE ECONOMIC AND SOCIAL RESEARCH COUNCIL (ESRC) 16–19 INITIATIVE

This was a major programme of research conducted between 1987 and 1989. It involved longitudinal surveys of representative samples of 16–19-year-olds in four contrasting areas—Kirkcaldy, Liverpool, Sheffield, and Swindon. Ethnographic inquiries were conducted alongside the larger-scale surveys.

The main strengths of this research were:

- It enabled the development of young people's lives to be related to characteristics of the areas where they lived.

- Considerable information was collected about the young people's attitudes and social lives, thus permitting exploration of the relationships between their careers in education and the labour market on the one hand, and their experiences and behaviour in their families and peer groups, and socio-political attitudes on the other.

The main report from this research is M. Banks *et al. Careers and Identities* (Open University Press, Milton Keynes, 1992).

The findings from the ethnographic studies are drawn together in a further book, I. Bates and G. Riseborough (eds.), *Youth and Inequality*, Open University Press, Buckingham, 1993).

The evidence from the ESRC 16–19 Initiative is used in all this book's chapters.

Hence the greater interest in not merely whether education and training in Britain meet British firms' requirements but how they perform against international standards. This is a particularly sensitive question in Britain because throughout most of the twentieth century the UK economy has grown more slowly than its main customers' and competitors'. From being the leading industrial nation and enjoying one of the world's highest standards of living, Britain has slipped down the economic league. Various explanations have been offered. Weaknesses in education and training are just among many contenders. Educators, trainers, and youth researchers may be predisposed towards these explanations because they lend importance to their activities. As previously stated, this book's position is one of sustained scepticism. Yet it is undeniable that the truth or falsehood of these explanations has become a matter of increasing national importance. This is because the internationalization of economic life could make it even more difficult than in the past for weaker national economies to hold their own except by holding down costs, including labour costs, which would mean living standards slipping further behind those in countries with more productive work-forces. It has become more vital for every country to have a world class work-force otherwise its companies stand to lose business and jobs. Multinationals will locate in places where the work-forces are either most productive or cheapest. Better educated and trained foreign workers could increasingly occupy the best jobs in Britain if the country failed to nurture equal talent.

There has been much interest in how vocational preparation in Britain compares with practices in the partner countries of the European Union, which are also our main competitors. There have been numerous studies, most of which conclude that young people in Britain are undereducated, undertrained, and underskilled compared with their counterparts in most other West European countries (Jarvis and Prais 1988; Prais and Wagner 1985; Steedman 1988). School-leavers in Britain are said to lag in mathematical skills, knowledge of science and technology, and certainly in foreign languages. Industrial training on the Continent is said to be geared to much higher standards than in Britain. Britain's academic élite may be world class but, it is claimed, at lower levels most other countries' achievements are superior. France retains most of its young people in full-time academic or vocational education until at least age 18. Germany has the vast majority of its 16–19-year-olds either in full-time education or in the dual system of apprentice training (part-time in industry and part-time in education). In most West European countries, and in the former communist societies, young people are separated into academic and technical or vocational tracks at least from age 14 or 15. Each track is said to provide an academic curriculum or vocational preparation appropriate to the abilities and interests of the young people who are recruited, who are then fed into related types of employment. Even though there has been a substantial expansion of post-16 education and training in Britain since the 1970s the gaps may not have closed. Other countries have not been standing still. Moreover, it has been argued that standards on Britain's recently introduced training schemes and vocational courses are much lower than on the continent. The Youth Training Scheme and National Vocational Qualifications have both been accused of perpetuating and consolidating low standards of vocational preparation (Ashton *et al.* 1989; Smithers 1993).

However, it may be misleading to generalize about the weaknesses, and any strengths, of vocational preparation throughout the length and breadth of the UK. There are some significant internal differences, especially between education and training in the UK's component countries. Northern Ireland still has an 11-plus and grammar schools in most parts of the province, the catholic–protestant division cuts through primary and secondary though not higher education, and the equivalent of Youth Training has been administered by central government rather than through local Training and Enterprise Councils. Scotland has a different set of school examinations from the rest of the UK. After passing O-levels academic pupils in Scotland can proceed to 'highers', which may be completed in just one year, after which the young people may enter higher education a year younger than when students in the rest of the UK typically enter, but first degree courses in Scottish universities traditionally require four years of full-time study. The Scottish system has a long history of retaining more 16-year-olds in full-time education, and carrying a higher proportion of the age group into higher education, than in England and Wales (Raffe and Courtenay 1988). In recent times Northern Ireland has also achieved higher rates of higher education enrolment than England and Wales. Allegations of relatively low standards compared with the rest of Europe should perhaps be targeted at England and Wales rather than the whole of Britain or the UK.

However the various parts of the UK compare with the rest of Europe, how Europe compares with the rest of the world has become an equally vital question. Will even the best European systems of education and training produce work-forces that match those of recently industrialized countries, particularly the so-called Asian tigers of the Pacific rim? Since the 1970s European companies have tried to emulate Japanese methods of lean production and total quality management. Higher education participation in some North Pacific countries is well ahead of

Europe's levels. If and when Britain provides higher education for 40 per cent of its young people the country will still trail South Korea by a wide margin. The recent changes that have occurred in transitions into the work-force in Britain could be leaving the country further behind other industrial societies than previously. As noted earlier, the reproduction of any work-force is a problem-strewn process. There will be little comfort in Britain successfully reproducing a second or third class work-force.

The entry into employment is a field in which policy failures can have expensive and very long-term consequences. As we have seen, there has been considerable state intervention in this area in Britain during the last twenty years. The rhetoric of, and actual government measures to deregulate the labour market, have coincided with greater than ever levels of state intervention in education and training. Billions of pounds sterling from public funds have been invested in new forms of vocational preparation in schools, colleges, and industry. Effective interventions that fulfilled their architects' hopes would have strengthened the economy, led to the creation of more attractive jobs for young people, and higher living standards for the entire population. Policy failures have equally profound implications—lifelong implications for individuals who enter adulthood without the skills and qualifications needed to obtain good jobs—and they are unlikely to be the only losers from policies that do not deliver on their promises.

The following chapters present the evidence on which recent policies can be judged. Chapter Two looks in greater detail at how the UK economy has changed in recent years and the implications for different groups of young people. Chapter Three considers the operation of recently created routes into the work-force as regards who gets which jobs, while Chapter Four deals with the implications of recent changes for occupational socialization. Although much has changed these chapters emphasize the continuities. Chapter Five presents some recent thinking on exactly how transitions have changed in recent years. According to one body of opinion, the most significant changes have been that transitions into the work-force have become more individualized and risk laden for all groups of young people.

Further reading

The main publication from the Economic and Social Research Council's 16–19 Initiative gives a good account of the new conditions facing present-day school-leavers. M. Banks, I. Bates, G. Breakwell, J. Bynner, N. Emler, L. Jamieson and K. Roberts (1992), *Careers and Identities*, Open University Press, Milton Keynes. A. Furlong (1992), *Growing Up in a Classless Society?*, Edinburgh University Press, Edinburgh, uses evidence from the Scottish Young People's Survey to describe how school-leavers' opportunities have changed since the 1970s.

Chapter Two

Economic Change and Young People

Exactly how Britain's economy has changed in recent years, and why it has failed to change as rapidly or in the ways that some would have wished, are very important questions that are really beyond the scope of this book. However, it is necessary to establish what the main changes have been in order to understand the trends in young people's job prospects.

As in many areas of sociology, very few 'facts' are generally agreed. This applies even when discussing exactly how the economy, and levels and patterns of employment, have changed. Needless to say, there is even greater controversy as to why certain changes have occurred and how things might have been different had there been a different UK government, or had the government adopted different policies. There is no dispute about some facts, like there being fewer jobs in manufacturing firms today than in the 1970s. There is less agreement on how the character of the jobs that have been preserved, and the new jobs that have been created, differ from those that have been lost or replaced. In particular, there is a fierce debate on whether jobs in general have been upgraded or whether the overall trend has been towards deskilling. Are the jobs awaiting school-leavers better or worse in the 1990s compared with the 1960s?

This controversy might appear capable of simple resolution. After all, social researchers have decades of experience in placing the work-force into different occupational 'boxes'; skilled, semi-skilled, and unskilled manual jobs, clerical and other white-collar grades. From census data it might appear simple to establish whether there are more highly skilled jobs today than in the past. The truth, however, is that social reality is rarely as straightforward as it can appear in tables of statistics. The problem is that jobs bearing the same titles are not necessarily the same today as several decades ago. Indeed, the same title can be applied to very different jobs at any one time. Teachers, for example, do not all do exactly the same job, and over time all teaching jobs have changed. Syllabuses have changed. So have the age profiles of pupils and students. Staff–student ratios in some sectors of education, particularly further and higher education, are very different from what they were in the 1960s. There have been equivalent changes in most parts of the economy.

Evidence from young people can be a good guide to exactly how employment has been changing. This is because young people are usually the first age group to feel the full force of any trends. The previous chapter explained why young people have normally been especially vulnerable in times of rising unemployment. Conversely, when new jobs are created these are particularly likely to be filled by young people. Apart from being available for recruitment, young people may have the additional advantage, in employers' eyes, of having no prior experience of outdated skills and work practices, and being easily trained for new types of employment.

A theme of this book is that it is often misleading to generalize about all young people and much the same can be said about trends in employment. It would be amazing if the same trend—upgrading or deskilling for example—had occurred in all sections of the economy and in all occupations. Another complication is that the same trend can appear differently depending on whose point of view is taken. For instance, there may be grounds for applauding the fact that on average workers in virtually all occupations today are better qualified than their predecessors. This could mean that the work-force at all levels has become more skilled and productive. However, from employees' positions this trend will have meant that they are gaining lower rewards for their qualifications in terms of levels of employment. Or, to put the point another way, it has become necessary to earn more qualifications than in the past to enter any level of employment.

A more highly skilled work-force?

The upgrading thesis is based on two kinds of evidence. The first is about the distribution of the work-force between occupational strata. There has been a long-term and ongoing trend towards a decline in the proportion of low level (manual) jobs and an increase in the proportion at higher (non-manual) levels. The sources of this trend lie in industry shifts and occupation shifts. *Industry shifts* are changes in the proportions of jobs in different economic sectors. Specifically, as regards upgrading, the proportion of all jobs which are in manufacturing industries, which employ large numbers of manual workers, has declined, while the proportion of employment in services, some of which contain much heavier concentrations of high level jobs—central and local government, health and education, financial and business services, for example—has increased. *Occupation shifts* are changes on the proportions of jobs at different levels within the same industries. Technological change has often been involved in these shifts. In manufacturing new technology has often mechanized manual occupations and reduced employment in these grades while creating a need for more qualified staff to design, manage, and maintain the new technical systems.

The second, more contested, source of upgrading concerns changes within occupations. It is argued that jobs at all levels have tended to become more demanding. Again, technological change is often said to have played a part. In professional, management, clerical, and manual occupations the technology that staff have to operate has become more advanced and is often said to require higher level skills than former work practices. It is also claimed that more intensive domestic and international competition has required businesses to become more efficient, which has led to jobs at all levels becoming heavier and more demanding. The craft grades in many firms have been multi-skilled; former demarcations between separate trades have been obliterated. Production staff in manufacturing and clerical employees in all business sectors have been required to work in teams and acquire the skills to cover each other's absences. Entire levels have been eliminated from management in some companies as the firms have endeavoured to become lean, efficient, and competitive. There is plenty of evidence of all these trends. Employees in all grades are more likely to report that their jobs have become more skilled than less skilled (Gallie and White 1993).

These are the trends in employment that lead to fears and claims that Britain's work-force is lagging behind occupational requirements. The government view has been that these trends will continue and that, despite the recent growth in the numbers of young people in education and training, further progress is needed not just to keep up but to catch up with change in the economy. Hence the Employment Department's targets: all 18-year-olds to have the opportunity to achieve Level 2 NVQs and 50 per cent to be achieving Level 3 (the A-level equivalent) by 1995 (Employment Department 1993). It was this scenario of increasing skill requirements that led to the late 1980s' warnings about a demographic time bomb (National Economic Development Office 1988).

Forecasts for rising skill requirements lend urgency to fears of Britain lagging behind competitor countries in the levels to which its young people are educated and trained. It has been argued that British firms are handicapped because German, French, Dutch, Japanese, and many other countries' workers are simply better (Jarvis and Prais 1988; Mason and Van Ark 1993; Prais and Wagner 1985). Some writers have argued that British businesses are forced into low skill, low cost, low wage strategies because they are unable to recruit sufficient quality labour to turn the businesses into high skill, high value added, high wage enterprises. Commentators who accept this diagnosis sometimes propose radical remedies like prohibiting the full-time employment of under-19-year olds (Layard 1992) and retaining the entire age group in schools and colleges (Cassels 1990).

Deskilling

There is a deskilling or degradation thesis which takes a contrary view of the trends. This thesis was originally formulated by Harry Braverman (1974) in the book *Labour and Monopoly Capital*. This book's central claim is that under capitalism there is an inevitable and relentless drive to extract more and more surplus value from labour, which is achieved by subjecting the labour process to stricter control. Braverman alleged a long-term trend towards separating the conception and execution of work tasks. In other words, employers and their agents do the thinking while workers simply offer labour power. A related alleged trend is towards tighter control over labour, which may be achieved through technology as more jobs become machine paced and monitored. Braverman argued that despite the talk and even genuine enthusiasm among managers for improving human relations and the quality of working life, the actual long-term trend was towards jobs being degraded. He believed that this trend was most advanced in manual occupations where former crafts had been deskilled, and that more recently it had spread into offices and would progressively change the jobs of many managers and professionally graded staff.

Few subsequent writers have felt able to accept that there is a long-term trend towards deskilling throughout the occupational structures in all capitalist economies. In Britain it is easy to find examples of deskilling, particularly in former craft occupations. There is also recent evidence of many traditionally non-skilled manual and office jobs being degraded by making the employees part-time, eroding any job security that they once possessed and holding their rates of pay well beneath average levels. However, it is easier to account for these trends in terms of particular kinds of technical change, especially as regards the deskilling of former crafts, and labour market conditions and government policies in the 1980s and early 1990s as regards the terms and conditions of employment of non-skilled manual and clerical staff, than a ubiquitous long-term degradation process.

However, without endorsing its polar opposite it is possible to list several strong objections to the upskilling thesis. It can be accused of making exaggerated claims, ignoring contrary evidence, and sometimes arguing without any solid evidence whatsoever. First, it is very easy to exaggerate the proportion of young people who might expect to benefit from occupational upgrading. The proportion of jobs in the so-called service class, the higher grade non-manual occupations, has certainly risen over time. After the Second World War around one-in-seven males were employed in these grades. By the 1980s this proportion had risen to over one-in-four (Goldthorpe *et al.* 1987). There had been a substantial increase. The proportion of males with jobs at these higher levels had more than doubled. Even so, these jobs are still a minority, and there is no chance of most male employees, not to mention females, holding such jobs. There will never be a time when most workers will have above average incomes and status. This is a statistical impossibility. Most young people are not destined to become brain surgeons, airline pilots, chartered accountants, or occupants of other jobs with the same status that the former have enjoyed up to now.

Secondly, the pace at which young people have become better qualified in recent years has been faster than any occupational upgrading. Young people in Britain have not been lagging behind but have moved ahead of occupational trends. The last chapter described how school-leavers have become better qualified. Success rates in GCSE examinations have risen and more young people have been remaining in education to gain further qualifications. So the entry requirements for jobs at virtually all levels have risen. Some occupations that were once open to 18- and even 16-year-olds are now being graduatized (Pike *et al.* 1992). Accountancy, law, and professional engineering are examples. Rather than a shortage of applicants with the customary entry qualifications, growing numbers of young people have been unable to find jobs for which their qualifications are required or where their certificated abilities will be used. Rather than finding themselves in high demand, more and more qualified young people have been experiencing the so-called 'great training robbery' (Berg 1973). The surplus of well-qualified labour on the market has enabled employers to select, and even insist upon qualifications that often bear little relationship to the jobs' technical requirements. Employers may recruit the well qualified simply because they are available; they are often regarded as the most able even when the content of their courses and training bears no relationship to the demands of the occupations that are being filled. Hence the alleged spread of a 'diploma disease', where qualified incompetents keep the talented but unqualified out of more and more jobs (Dore 1976).

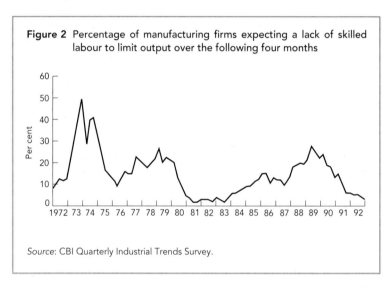

Figure 2 Percentage of manufacturing firms expecting a lack of skilled labour to limit output over the following four months

Source: CBI Quarterly Industrial Trends Survey.

Thirdly, in his review of the topic Shackleton (1993) concludes that there is no hard, or any other clear evidence that British firms are handicapped by their inability to recruit skilled and qualified staff, or suffer from using undereducated and undertrained personnel in key occupations. At the end of the 1980s, after eight years of continuous economic growth, most firms did not report recruitment difficulties or skill deficits, the proportion of firms reporting such problems was no higher than in the 1970s, and only a minority of the firms that reported any difficulties said that their production had been hindered (IFF Research 1990). This evidence is summarized in Figure 2. In any case, their meanings are not always clear when employers complain of shortages of skilled and appropriately qualified applicants. They may mean that recruiters have less choice than they would prefer. Or they may mean that the individuals recruited have to be trained up to the required levels. If skill shortages are a problem in Britain they seem to be the kind of problem that most businesses are able to solve. Large firms are the least likely to report skill shortages and recruitment difficulties (IFF Research 1993; Roberts and Corcoran-Nantes 1994). Most of the complaints are from smaller businesses and it can be argued that in any market economy the weaker firms will always have the greatest difficulties, whether in attracting investment, selling their goods, or hiring labour.

Fourthly, even if other countries give their young people more years of education and training than Britain, it will not necessarily follow that the other countries' way is the only way or even the best way of producing an international class work-force. Compared with young Germans, young people in Britain spend less time in full-time education and formal training programmes and are less likely to earn higher level academic qualifications and vocational qualifications at all levels. However, Britain's young people gain the earlier experience in employment, where they pick up more uncertificated skills than young Germans acquire in their organized programmes (Bynner and Roberts 1991). The result is that German employers find it relatively easy to recruit adults with certificated skills, but British employers benefit from the huge reservoir of uncertificated talent that is available for hire and capable of being trained up to the levels and in the particular skills that employers need.

Fifthly, if more British than German (and French and Dutch) firms are using low skill, low cost, low wage production strategies, the reason will not necessarily be that British workers are insufficiently educated and trained to be turned into highly productive employees in capital intensive businesses. An alternative explanation could be that the low wage, low cost strategy is easier to operate in Britain, which is one of the few European Union countries without any minimum wage legislation and whose government in recent years has preached the virtues of labour market deregulation. Another alternative explanation is cultural; that the time and manner in which Britain became the first industrial nation resulted in the preservation of many features of the traditional aristocratic culture which have subsequently suppressed the status of technical education, training, and skills (Weiner 1981).

A sixth objection to the upskilling thesis is that its arguments construct an ideological smoke-screen which blames young people, and sometimes their parents and teachers also, while concealing the real sources of the country's economic difficulties (Bates *et al.* 1984; Finn 1987; Loney 1979; Rees and Atkinson 1982). Governments and employers have vested interests in shifting the blame. Education and training have the added political attraction of being areas in which it is fairly easy, though not inexpensive, for governments to intervene and produce tangible results in terms of the numbers on schemes and courses. Other types of economic intervention tend to be more hazardous in their outcomes. Allegations that the economy needs more youth education and training are now echoed by the substantial numbers of trainers and teachers with vested interests in the prescription (Shackleton 1993). It is always tempting to support even a weak argument when one's own job and career prospects could be at stake.

Restructuring

Apart from any overall upskilling or deskilling, Britain's economy has been undergoing other kinds of restructuring which have had clearer effects on young people's prospects.

Sector shifts

First, manufacturing employment has been declining since the 1950s and this trend is continuing. Countries such as Britain are often referred to as industrial societies. It may still be correct to treat manufacturing as the base on which the country's export performance and most other types of employment and general prosperity depend. However, manufacturing firms have never been responsible for most jobs. Currently they employ less than a quarter of the work-force and this share is declining. Manufacturing output has not fallen. The decline in employment which has occurred in all Britain's main manufacturing sectors has been due to improved labour productivity, which in turn has usually owed much to new technology. Levels of output and sales by manufacturing firms are more crucial than employment for the strength of the wider economy. Nevertheless, most people's wages are not earned by manufacturing. Most jobs, well over two-thirds, are now in service sectors.

This shift of employment into services was noted in connection with the upskilling thesis when examples were given of service sectors with top-heavy occupational profiles—education and health for example. This makes it all the more important to note that hospitals and schools employ cleaners as well as doctors and teachers, and some service sectors where there has been particularly strong employment growth since the 1970s have bottom-heavy job profiles. Restaurants, hotels, other catering establishments, and tourism related businesses are prime examples.

The decline of manufacturing jobs has meant that school- and college-leavers have become less likely to find employment at all levels in manufacturing, and more likely to obtain jobs in services. It may be vital for Britain's economic future that manufacturers obtain the supplies of appropriately qualified labour that they need but it remains the case that young people's chances of obtaining such employment have declined, and, in all probability, will continue to do so.

Hours of work

Alongside the above sector shift there has been a decline in the proportion of full-time jobs and a substantial increase in the number of part-time occupations. Many of the service sector jobs that have been created since the 1970s have been part-time. During the late 1980s when unemployment was declining and new jobs were being created, most of the expansion was in part-time employment. There was no net growth in full-time jobs. Hence the controversy about whether Britain's economy has been generating more employment overall or whether we have entered an era of net jobless growth. At the end of the 1980s the number of people employed in Britain reached a record level but if the employment level was measured in terms of the total number of hours worked there had been a net decline during the 1980s. The shift towards part-time work has favoured sections of the work-force that are most likely to seek part-time employment. Married women are the obvious example. Meanwhile, groups seeking full-time jobs, which include most school- and college-leavers, have found their employment opportunities shrinking.

The sex balance

The proportion of females in Britain's work-force has been rising. By the early 1990s women were over 45 per cent of all employees. This trend has been partly due to broader changes in women's roles and aspirations—more have wanted and have been available for employment—and partly to the shifts in employment noted above. Much of the recent growth has been in occupations where female employment is traditional—nursing, teaching, and restaurant and supermarket jobs for example. The most spectacular declines in employment have been in occupations which men have traditionally dominated, namely, manual jobs in manufacturing and extractive industries. One might have expected these trends to make it easier for female school-leavers, and more difficult for males, to find employment, except that young women have faced fiercer competition from the older females who have been re-entering the labour force or holding on to their employment in growing numbers. Also, most of the new women's employment has been part-time.

Regional differences

A complication is that the gains and losses of different kinds of employment have not always occurred in the same parts of the country. Redundant steelworkers in South Wales would have experienced difficulty in obtaining employment as money market traders even if the latter jobs had been close to their homes, but in practice job losses and job creation rarely occur in the same neighbourhoods. Closures of steelworks, coal mines, and shipyards have typically left redundant workers stranded in high unemployment areas.

There are wide geographical differences within the UK in levels of employment and unemployment, and in the types of employment that are available. So adults' and young people's opportunities vary considerably according to where they live. However, regional differences in levels of unemployment were narrower in the recession of the early 1990s than in the early 1980s when they were narrower than in the 1930s. The reason is that, over time, most regions have acquired more balanced economies. There are now fewer towns, cities, and regions that are dependent on single firms and industries. Also, the population is more mobile. More workers have private motor cars which widen their personal labour markets, and more people own their own homes, which makes relocation not necessarily easy or simple but a more viable option than when families occupy rented accommodation. Selling and buying are usually more straightforward than obtaining an equivalent rented dwelling in another part of the country.

Another difference between the geography of employment in the 1990s compared with earlier decades is that there has been a trend in all regions for jobs to move out of cities and into small towns or city outskirts industrial estates. Firms find it easier to obtain land on which to build and expand outside the major cities. Road access is normally easier on greenfield sites, and out-of-town workplaces today are often more accessible than city centres for employees who prefer to travel to work in their motor cars. The consequences of the decline in employment in Britain's major cities in recent times have been similar to the decline of entire regions in former decades. Inner-city residents, especially those without private motor transport, have seen their local employment prospects deteriorate, while in some former rural areas labour demand has become buoyant.

Young people's prospects, therefore, have continued to vary depending on their places of residence. This has been emphasized by David Ashton and his colleagues (1982, 1986) following their studies of the youth labour markets in Leicester, St Albans and Sunderland. Within each of these areas unemployment was highest among the least qualified young people who tended to be from working-class families. Sociologists are accustomed to stressing the importance of these predictors. Maybe it is easy to understand why sociologists have sometimes overlooked the significance of geography. In Ashton's research young people from working-class families in St Albans were more likely to obtain non-manual jobs than middle-class youth in Sunderland.

Flexibility

A trend towards work-force flexibility is said to have cross-cut all other types of restructuring. Flexibility is said to have become imperative for successful businesses on account of their increasingly volatile environments. Technological change is one source of volatility. Its sheer pace with forever shorter cycles means that firms must be adaptable. Fiercer competition with the internationalization of production and marketing is a further alleged destabilizing development.

Two types of flexibility have been distinguished. First there is functional flexibility, which is said to be demanded of core, skilled, permanent workers. They need to be adaptable, capable of keeping abreast of technological changes and switching to new jobs according to changes in their companies' requirements. Numerical flexibility is the second type which, it is claimed, is typically sought when hiring less skilled labour. By employing part-time staff, temporary workers, and casuals, and by using subcontractors, businesses can change their size and shape from year to year, month to month, and even according to the time of the day.

The trend towards flexibility in employment is sometimes portrayed as one aspect of a transition to a post-Fordist economy. In the Fordist era large firms offered security to their staff. Their size gave these firms the strength to be able to reward their staff with greater security than small businesses. Different grades of labour were hired and trained to perform specialist tasks. The craft grades learnt their skills as apprentices and practised them until retirement. The man on the assembly line could earn a living for as long as he could stand the pace and monotony. The firms and their work-forces were among the more stable fixtures in the socio-economic landscape whereas the flexible firm theory suggests that we are now into 'new times'.

An implication of this shift in firms' strategies is said to be a clearer division of the work-force into core and peripheral, or primary and secondary employees. Primary workers are typically well qualified, trained, skilled, and enjoy the greater security and higher pay. Secondary labour is less qualified, less trained, lower paid, and has minimal if any job security. There have always been inequalities in employment but recent trends are said to favour even greater *dualism* or *segmentation* between 'good jobs' and 'trash jobs', and therefore between primary workers and second-class employees. As with all kinds of restructuring—between business sectors, full-time and part-time, men's and women's jobs, and between geographical areas—there are winners and losers from increased flexibility. At any rate, the gains and losses are not distributed equally. The particular implication for young people of a broader trend towards a clearer division between core and peripheral workers will be to make it all the more important for individuals to establish themselves in primary employment early in their careers otherwise they may be at risk of long-term confinement to poor quality jobs.

Unemployment

An outcome of all the restructuring that has taken place has been higher unemployment than in the 1950s and 60s, and young workers have been the most vulnerable age group. There are several reasons for young people's exceptional vulnerability which were noted in the previous chapter.

Unemployment has been one of the reasons for young people staying longer in full-time education and progressing through training schemes. In Scotland a 'discouraged worker effect' has been discovered with stay-on rates in education rising particularly strongly in areas with the highest unemployment (Raffe and Willms 1989). In England and Wales it has been impossible to isolate any such effect on retention rates in education in the evidence from the Youth Cohort Surveys (Gray *et al.* 1992), but this does not mean that there have been no discouraged workers in schools and colleges south of the border. Rather, other developments encouraging higher retention rates in education will have overwhelmed the effects of local unemployment rates. Prolonged careers in education are associated with success in secondary schools and middle-class family backgrounds. So the highest stay-on rates are among young people from families with the least experience of, and who themselves are the least at risk of, unemployment on entering the labour market.

Irrespective of labour market conditions, there has been a long-term trend towards longer careers in education in all industrial societies. A generation ratchet effect seems to operate. Most parents want their children to be at least as successful in education as they were themselves. Each successive generation therefore has slightly higher educational aspirations than its predecessor. However, during particular historical periods the trend towards longer careers in education has accelerated, and in recent years the high level of youth unemployment has been an accelerating factor. Yet despite the massive transfer of young people off the labour market and into education and training, unemployment has remained a major problem in most parts of the UK, and a particularly serious threat facing young people even after their prolonged education and training. By the mid-1990s unemployment among university graduates had become a major problem.

Disaggregating young people

Unravelling the implications of recent economic trends for young people is a complicated exercise. First, it is necessary to unpackage the various trends in the economy in order to make each comprehensible. Secondly, in order to identify the implications it is necessary to realize that the trends have not occurred in splendid isolation. They have occurred simultaneously though not universally, and have produced different configurations of opportunities in different places. Some areas have suffered particularly sharp losses of manufacturing jobs, sometimes but not always alongside a growth of service sector employment, sometimes in high level occupations but often in low level part-time jobs. All the trends have been nationwide but their strength has varied from place to place, and every local labour market has distinctive features. Thirdly, it is necessary to disaggregate young people. They share some things on account of their age. For example, young people always tend to be fully exposed to whatever trends occur in the labour market. However, young people are as clearly divided as adults and the implications of any trend or configuration in local job opportunities are never exactly the same for everyone in the age group. This can be illustrated by examining in more detail the implications of place of residence, gender, and school-leaving qualifications, exploring the interactive effects of these divisions, and then looking at the significance of the growth in part-time employment.

Place

We have seen how Ashton's research in Leicester, St Albans, and Sunderland drew attention to inter-area differences in school-leavers' job opportunities. Young people's job prospects depend on their qualifications and other personal qualities, but also on where they happen to live. This has also been emphasized in the ESRC 16–19 Initiative (see page 25). In terms of economic conditions the extreme areas in this study were Swindon, one of the fastest growing towns in Europe in the 1980s, and Liverpool, where the labour market was chronically depressed. Table 6 traces the progress of young people in Swindon and Liverpool who completed the fifth year in their secondary schools in 1985. In Swindon over a quarter were able to make 'traditional transitions' straight from school into full-time jobs at age 16, compared with less than one in ten in Liverpool, where it was far more common for 16-year-olds who left school to enter the YTS. The reverse applied in Swindon; more 16-year-olds obtained jobs than passed through the YTS. Over the next two-and-a-half years more of the young people in both areas left education and the numbers in employment rose, but in Swindon the employment rate became 30 per cent higher than in Liverpool, where unemployment was far more prevalent.

The samples studied in the ESRC 16–19 Initiative were sufficiently large to permit various breakdowns, by educational qualifications for example, which shows that how much difference 'place' was making to the young people varied according to their educational attainments.

Table 6 1984–5 fifth formers in Swindon and Liverpool

| | Autumn 1985 | | Spring 1988 | |
| | Age 16 | | Age 18–19 | |
	Sw	L	Sw	L
Education	45	47	15	22
Schemes	18	34	—	1
Full-time job	28	8	73	45
Part-time job	5	2	4	7
Unemployed	3	9	4	22
Other	1	—	3	4

Source: Roberts *et al.* (1991).

Table 7 divides the Swindon and Liverpool samples into quartiles (equal sized quarters) according to their educational qualifications at age 16. Group 1 was the least qualified while group 4 was the best qualified. Qualifications were making a difference to the young people's career development wherever they lived. In both Liverpool and Swindon the best qualified were the most likely to remain in full-time education up to age 18–19. In both places the least qualified were the most likely to experience unemployment. Simultaneously, place was making a difference to the young people's career development whatever their qualifications. Among the better qualified, Liverpool had the highest rate of participation in full-time education at age 18–19. This was not because more of Liverpool's young people were progressing into higher education. There was little difference between Swindon and Liverpool in this respect. The higher participation in education among Liverpool's 18–19-year-olds was due to their greater likelihood of being in further education. Their Swindon counterparts were mostly in full-time jobs. The Swindon–Liverpool comparison reveals a clear discouraged worker effect. Using such extreme cases highlights this effect, which is easily lost when all parts of England and Wales are thrown into the analysis and the effects of local unemployment rates

Table 7 1984–5 fifth formers: educational qualifications and career development

	Positions, Spring 1988			
Swindon	1	2	3	4
	%	%	%	%
Education	—	3	5	34
YTS	—	—	—	—
Full-time job	79	84	85	89
Part-time job	5	—	6	4
Unemployed	14	7	2	1
Other	2	6	1	3
Liverpool	%	%	%	%
Education	2	9	20	49
YTS	3	1	—	1
Full-time job	35	59	60	36
Part-time job	8	7	4	2
Unemployed	51	22	13	5
Other	2	2	3	7

Source: Roberts *et al.* (1991).

are buried among the numerous additional factors that influence education stay-on rates. Place was making a difference to the career development of the better qualified, but it was making even more difference among the least qualified in Swindon and Liverpool. More of Liverpool's least qualified quartile were unemployed than in full-time jobs at age 18–19 whereas in Swindon roughly six times as many were in jobs as were unemployed.

Place makes the most difference to the least qualified young people. Those who succeed in secondary school are able to progress into higher education after which they typically seek jobs in the national labour market or, at any rate, in other areas apart from where they received their school education. Young people who leave school at age 16 or 17 and enter the labour market are more affected by the local labour market conditions, whatever these might be. Such young people are usually unable to relocate and widen their quests for employment. Few have any choice but to remain home based. Few 16- and 17-year-olds have the regular use of private motor vehicles so their employment opportunities are normally restricted to areas that can be reached from their homes by public transport.

This has led to suspicions that young people's employment prospects and risks of unemployment could depend not on the labour market conditions prevailing throughout their towns or cities, but within the particular districts where they live. Specifically, it has been hypothesized that inner-city youth may be especially disadvantaged as a result of the decline in employment in and close to city centres. Similarly, it has been suggested that young people who live on city fringe housing developments may experience exceptional job deprivation when businesses on the neighbouring industrial estates close down. In practice, however, the particular districts within town and cities where young people reside do not appear to make much difference to their employment prospects. There are town, city, and regional effects, but not district effects. The reasons why unemployment rates are particularly high in certain districts owe far more to the characteristics of their inhabitants—usually their lack of qualifications and skills—than the nearby employment opportunities (Garner et al. 1988).

Explaining the absence of neighbourhood or district effects requires a digression into how labour markets work. The Employment Department divides the country into local labour markets, which are supposed to be territories within which local employers and resident workers tend to concentrate their labour market behaviour. In practice, however, there are no clearly bounded local labour markets in modern Britain. Some residents in all cities commute to work in other towns and cities. Every individual has a unique personal labour market, meaning the territory within which he or she is willing to travel to work. The personal labour markets of individuals with the same address are not always identical. Car owners are able to search and travel more widely than individuals who depend on public transport. Some workers pursue careers that require a willingness to relocate to other parts of the country, and abroad in some instances. Most firms seek different categories of labour in different ways, so the territories from which they attempt to recruit are likely to vary according to the types of jobs being filled. For example, a firm may advertise locally to fill clerical jobs but nationally when management vacancies arise. The many occupational labour markets within which most employers recruit, and the numerous personal labour markets of workers, diverge but intersect to an extent that usually eliminates district or neighbourhood effects. Simultaneously, there is sufficient overlap in the labour markets of workers and employers in any town or city to create a town or city labour market effect. This means that residents in Toxteth are handicapped in their search for work by the depressed state of the Liverpool economy rather than a particular shortage of jobs in Toxteth itself. Conversely, it was the buoyancy of the Swindon labour market, not the levels of employment in the particular neighbourhoods where they lived, that was responsible for young people in Swindon facing much lower risks of unemployment than their Liverpool counterparts in the late 1980s.

Gender

Here the main social fact for sociology to explain is that most males and females still end up in gender typical occupations. Males dominate in management and high status professions while women do most of the clerical jobs. Most skilled manual workers are male while women do most of the lower status and lower paid work in supermarkets, hotels, and restaurants. In hospitals most consultants (senior doctors) are male while most nurses are female. In factories that produce electrical goods men usually install and maintain the machinery while women do the light, nimble, and monotonous assembly work. The equal pay and equal opportunity legislation of the 1970s seems to have made hardly any difference. Technical and occupational changes have been absorbed within patriarchal workplace relationships. When information technology began to spread in offices and factories the familiar gender divisions were reproduced; men usually controlled while women operated the equipment (Cockburn 1991).

Some things have changed. Males' and females' different experiences in the labour market used to be preceded by education in which, although girls led at primary school, they were subsequently overtaken and outperformed by boys. A vast literature was generated on the ways in which schools were unfriendly to girls. By the mid-1990s the reality in education had made the literature look outdated. Girls had become the educational achievers (see Figure 3). They were maintaining their primary school lead over boys throughout secondary and into higher education. Girls today outperform boys in GCSE, do better at A-levels, and are more likely to enter higher education. Girls have also been making inroads into traditionally male subjects. They now do better than boys in GCSE maths and are a growing proportion of sixth form and higher education students in science and medicine. More young women than men are currently in medical schools training to be doctors.

It is possible only to speculate on the likely reasons for these recent changes. First, the legislation of the 1970s may be making a delayed

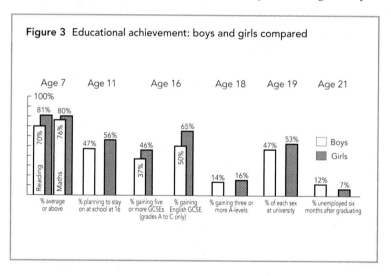

Figure 3 Educational achievement: boys and girls compared

impact. There was probably always going to be a *cultural lag* before attitudes changed and women began taking advantage of their legal rights to equal pay and other opportunities. Secondly, recent female school-leavers have been the first cohorts, most of whose mothers held paid employment for the greater part of their daughters' lives. Many members of these recent cohorts will also have learnt from personal experience that marriage no longer guarantees lifetime economic security. Thirdly, parents and teachers now believe that it is just as important for girls as for boys to achieve all that they are able. It is impossible to isolate the effects of 'Girls can do it' and other campaigns supported by the Equal Opportunities Commission. In recent years these initiatives have been moving with broader historical tides. There are few remnants anywhere of the old view that educational success matters most for sons. Female school-leavers now attach the same importance to occupational careers as males (Roberts and Chadwick 1991). Any earlier tendency for boys to seek employment careers while girls sought husbands has been completely obliterated. Fourthly, girls seem to have been turning their feminine characteristics to their educational advantage. Boys are the more likely to play truant and behave in ways leading to their exclusion from schools.

In the labour market the changes have been far less dramatic. There have been changes but these have been uneven and have made only a marginal difference in a work-force that is still composed of occupations most of which are mainly male or mainly female. Boys and girls still tend to enter masculine and feminine jobs, and are prepared for such jobs on training schemes. Gender divisions are much more pronounced on vocationally specialized courses than in academic education (Blackman 1987; Brown 1987; Buchmann and Charles 1992). Male school- and scheme-leavers still tend to enter jobs in which they receive longer training, leading to faster and higher rising careers than females. At age 16–17 there is little difference in the earnings of employed males and females but by age 19–20 the males are pushing ahead (Roberts and Parsell 1991). Employers are still reluctant to train young women who are expected to interrupt their careers on becoming parents (Ashton *et al.* 1982; Roberts *et al.* 1987). Girls who enter male occupations are expected to pursue continuous full-time careers, like men, if they want genuinely equal opportunities (Roberts and Corcoran-Nantes 1995). Even female school-leavers who say that they want careers are mostly resigned to acquiring male partners who will be unwilling to share the child care and other domestic work equally (Chisholm and du Bois-Reymond 1993). Men's lives and attitudes have been changing more slowly than women's. In recent years the Equal Opportunities Commission has been handling a rising number of complaints from men who have tried unsuccessfully to enter female occupations. However, very few young men aspire to women's jobs. It is far easier to identify young women who have broken into male occupations than young men who have taken up typing and other kinds of women's work (Roberts and Chadwick 1991). On entering the labour market young women tend to follow the line of least resistance even when this means compromising their ambitions. There is less difference in the sexes' aspirations than in their career expectations, and less difference in their expectations than in the types of employment that they actually enter (Roberts and Chadwick 1991).

Actually more young women have been entering hitherto mainly male professions. Moreover, more of these young women have been gaining post-entry professional qualifications, staying in the main career streams and taking maternity leave instead of terminating their employment. This has been happening in law, banking, and insurance, for example. On the basis of these trends Crompton and Sanderson (1986) have expressed cautious optimism that there will be a long-term trend towards sex equality in the labour market. Male dominance in education crumbled first, and maybe males' positions in the labour force will follow. Only time will finally tell, but even cautious optimism may prove over-optimistic. Not all of the women who enter hitherto male occupations remain in the main career streams (McRae *et al.* 1991). In any case, the young women who have broken in have been a minority of their sex. They are not statistically representative. Moreover, the clearest examples of females breaking in are all in high level occupations. These are occupations which have been expanding and, therefore, where it has been relatively easy to accommodate new-comers. The highly educated males and females who are recruited to these occupations tend to be more committed to sex equality than other members of their age group (Banks *et al.* 1992), and their jobs tend to be those where qualifications are most decisive in recruitment (Dench 1993). Young women have made fewer inroads into male craft occupations. These types of employment have been contracting. It has been easier for 16–18-year-old female school-leavers to obtain the types of jobs in which women have long dominated—in offices, shops, hotels, and restaurants. Women's presence in skilled manual occupations still tends to be 'token'.

However, it could be misleading to regard male school-leavers, especially those seeking manual employment, as the privileged sex. The skilled and other jobs in manufacturing that they formerly entered have been disappearing. There are far fewer craft apprentices today than in the 1960s. There are fewer opportunities to find work in factories, mines, and docks. Unqualified and poorly qualified young male school-leavers have been among the main victims of occupational restructuring. Male employment has declined and male school-leavers have felt the full force of this trend.

Their female counterparts have faced other problems. Breaking into traditionally male manual jobs has become more difficult in so far as the jobs have become scarcer. At the same time, young females have met growing competition from the rising number of older married women who have been re-entering or remaining in the labour market, and who are often regarded as more reliable and stable by employers who recruit to factory and office jobs. Also, much female employment is now part-time. Many of the occupations formerly entered by 16–18-year-old females have been fragmented. The net result has been similar levels of unemployment among young males and females (Banks *et al.* 1992).

A crucial point is that, like place of residence, gender does not have constant implications among all groups of young people. The significance of being male and female depends, among other things, on individuals' qualifications and, therefore, the types of employment to which they have access. Among the educationally successful the sexes' lives have become more similar in terms of their types of education, qualifications obtained, types of employment, and leisure activities also (Roberts *et al.* 1990). On the basis of her research on the Isle of Sheppey among 153 16-year-old school-leavers, Claire Wallace (1987) formulated a polarization thesis. She drew attention to how, as they embarked upon their labour market careers, young people from the same schools gradually grew apart. One type of polarization was between those who established themselves in jobs and others who became long-term or repeatedly unemployed. Among the latter she also drew attention to how the lives of the sexes were polarized. Young unemployed females do not typically decide that the solution to their problems is to 'get a man' (see also Griffin 1985). There tends to be an acute shortage of potential male breadwinners in such girls' social networks. Young unemployed females are more likely to stay at home with domestic commitments and no money. Some become single parents. Young unemployed males are unable to become family providers. The end result is wide social class differences within each sex according to whether individuals are successful or unsuccessful in education and the labour market, but the differences are especially wide among females. On the one hand, more young women than ever are entering high level occupations that were once almost exclusively male. Simultaneously, more young women have been confined to unemployment or poor quality jobs on the secondary side of the dual labour market.

Qualifications

Educational qualifications are the best of all predictors of young people's subsequent career development. Needless to say, qualifications are not perfect predictors. They do not guarantee employment. There is a wide spread of occupational attainment at all qualification levels. No employers recruit solely on the basis of qualifications. The importance attached to formal proof of educational attainment varies between occupations and employers. The latter usually say that personal qualities are at least as important. Even so, a given level of qualification may still be necessary in order to survive the initial sifts of applicants. Qualifications are sometimes used as indicators of personal qualities such as industriousness. Sometimes they are used simply as indicators of general ability. The attention that employers pay to educational qualifications is rarely based on a systematic appraisal of the fit between the syllabuses and the requirements of the jobs being filled. Nevertheless, qualifications are far and away the best assets with which young people can embark on their working lives. Family backgrounds influence young people's adult life chances mainly via their relationships with educational attainment. Nowadays the way in which parents are best able to give their children good starts in life is by ensuring that they are well educated.

Nevertheless, the value of qualifications varies. Obtaining the maximum, and sometimes any, labour market returns depends on having the qualifications at the right time. Secondary school qualifications work best at the point of school-leaving. There is little point, in terms of career advantages, in experienced workers studying for GCSEs or A-levels. Generally speaking, in terms of career returns, the sooner individuals gain qualifications the better. GCSEs obtained after age 16 can be devalued by the extra time spent studying for them (Roberts *et al.* 1987). Higher education qualifications work best for the young. When firms recruit graduates they nearly always expect the recruits to be in their twenties. The value of qualifications can also depend on being in the right place, meaning in a labour market situation where there are employers seeking the qualifications in question. Holding qualifications, or not having any at all, has different implications depending on the state of the local labour market. We saw earlier that leaving school with poor qualifications or none at all was far more likely to lead to unemployment in Liverpool than in Swindon in the late 1980s.

Returns on qualifications also vary by gender. Nowadays girls become better qualified than boys on average, but males still do better in the labour market. At all occupational levels females need to be better qualified than males in order to equal the latter's achievements. This means that women are usually better qualified than the men who are doing the same jobs.

The returns that young people can expect from their educational qualifications have also changed over time. Young people who progressed through higher education used to be rewarded with graduate jobs. Sixteen-year-olds with O-levels (the equivalent to today's higher grade GCSEs) used to have good chances of obtaining apprentice training, provided they were males. Nowadays so many young people succeed in higher education that the majority cannot obtain graduate jobs, that is, jobs for which a degree is an essential requirement. As more young people have obtained them, all qualifications have been occupationally devalued. The occupational rewards from a clutch of GCSEs, A-levels, or a degree are lower than in the past. However, the employment prospects of young people without qualifications have also deteriorated. Rather than resenting being confined to non-skilled jobs, unqualified school-leavers today are likely to feel successful or lucky if they obtain such employment. The penalty for educational failure today is often 'no job' rather than poor quality employment. The value of all types of qualifications may have declined, but the gap between the best and least qualified's prospects is as wide as ever.

Part-time jobs

The rise in part-time and the decline in the number of full-time jobs has been bad news for school-leavers seeking full-time employment, while simultaneously permitting high levels of part-time working and earning among pupils and students. Attitudes towards students taking paid jobs in the evenings, weekends, and vacations have changed since the 1960s. The employment of schoolchildren was once deplored at educational conferences and surrounded by swathes of protective legislation dating back to the nineteenth century, when the battle commenced to exclude young children from coal mines and factories. The remnants of child employment—school pupils with newspaper and milk delivery rounds—were regularly criticized by teachers and other educationalists, and there were intermittent campaigns against the employment of children on fairgrounds and in other tourism related businesses. Working children tended to be low achievers at school and were usually from working-class homes (Roberts 1967). Teachers generally agreed that pupils should concentrate on their studies. The same attitude presided in higher education. Universities had rules prohibiting students from taking paid jobs during the terms, and vacations were considered best kept for reading and other forms of study.

Since the 1960s there has been a sea change. Most young people now gain experience of paid work before completing their secondary education. Part-time employment is now as common among students from middle-class as working-class homes. Those who continue in education for the longest are the most likely to take part-time jobs. This behaviour is now encouraged by teachers and parents who see part-time employment as a means of giving young people a measure of financial independence and satisfying their consumer aspirations while they continue with their studies. In the USA the student working his or her way through high school and college has a long history as a cultural hero and this culture has now spread into Britain.

The England and Wales Youth Cohort Survey found that over a half of third and fourth year secondary school pupils had part-time jobs in 1983–4. In 1990 Hutson and Cheung (1991) surveyed 334 sixth form and tertiary college students in Swansea and found that 66 per cent were working part-time, mainly in Saturday jobs. In a subsequent 1992 survey among South Wales and Bromley (south London) sixth formers, Hutson (1992) found that in Bromley three-quarters of both sexes, and in South Wales three-quarters of the girls and half of the boys, had Saturday jobs, mostly in retailing. In 1993 Riskowski's study of 116 students at Epping Forest College found that 63 per cent had regular part-time jobs at the time of the survey and 91 per cent had done some paid work during the previous year. The ESRC 16–19 Initiative also found high levels of part-time employment among 16–19-year-old students. Part-time work accounted for roughly a half of the young people's incomes (Roberts and Parsell 1991). Many were earning more at weekends than the allowances paid to full-time youth trainees. This meant that remaining in full-time education beyond age 16 was losing its association with sacrificing income and immediate consumption. Only the 16- and 17-year-olds with conventional full-time jobs, not youth trainees or the unemployed, had incomes and spending levels superior to the students. The declining value of the grants available to higher education students has meant that increasing numbers who are nominally studying full-time are in practice working their way through college.

The spread of part-time work is another clear example of the same occupational trend having entirely different implications for different groups of young people. Easier access to part-time jobs has made it possible or more attractive for young people to continue in post-compulsory education by reducing the financial penalties that would otherwise have been incurred. One result is that today's post-compulsory students tend to be a time pressured group. George Riseborough's (1993*a*) ethnographic study of Sheffield students on a BTEC course in hotel and catering management produced several examples of students with extremely long total work weeks. Simultaneously, earlier school-leavers' chances of obtaining full-time jobs have declined. Many have experienced unemployment while some, mainly females, have accepted part-time jobs. Some have constructed early working lives from a succession of part-time jobs, some done simultaneously and others consecutively.

The balance sheet

It is impossible to present a simple balance sheet revealing what young people have lost and gained as a result of recent economic changes. This is partly because the changes themselves have been complicated. There have been several kinds of restructuring—shifts in employment between business sectors, occupational levels, and parts of the country. Simultaneously, some jobs have become more skilled while others have been deskilled. The picture is further complicated by the net effects being different for different groups of young people defined by various combinations of gender, qualifications, and place of residence. Generalizations about trends in the prospects of all males or all females, or all young people in given localities, are usually wrong.

The best candidates as major beneficiaries from the overall trends are well-qualified females with access, either on account of their places of residence or their mobility, to workplaces where additional management and professionally graded jobs have been created, usually in service industries. While pursuing their qualifications these young women have become better able to support their lifestyles by taking part-time jobs. However, the nomination of these females as winners is a relative judgement. They are still less successful in the labour market in terms of their types of employment, levels of pay, and promotion prospects than equally qualified men. Moreover, members of both sexes who enter high level jobs will usually have needed to study for longer and obtain more qualifications than would have been necessary in the past, and the work pressures in the jobs themselves will often have become more intense. Nevertheless, such young people's grounds for complaint look trivial when compared with trends in the job prospects of poorly qualified males and females in the parts of Britain where restructuring has meant heavy job losses and high unemployment. Males in such areas have often seen the manual jobs in manufacturing (or coal mines or shipyards) that they could formerly have entered either disappear or be upgraded to technician or technologist level and thereby pushed beyond their own reach. The females have often found their former full-time, relatively secure jobs disintegrating into part-time, temporary, and low paid positions for which the young females have been competing with older women. The quality of the available jobs, from the points of view of such young people, is more likely to appear part of the problem rather than an acceptable solution to their labour market difficulties.

Further reading

D. Ashton, M. J. Maguire and M. Spillsbury (1989), *Re-structuring the Labour Market: the Implications for Youth*, Macmillan, London, offers an excellent overview of the main trends in the UK economy and their implications for young people. For a graphic account of the difficulties confronting young people attempting to be enterprising in a chronically depressed region, see R. MacDonald and F. Coffield (1991), *Risky Business? Youth and the Enterprise Culture*, Falmer Press, Lewes. C. D. Wallace (1987) *For Richer, For Poorer*, Tavistock, London, uses her evidence from research on the Isle of Sheppey to unravel the different implications of economic trends for males and females from different social class backgrounds.

Chapter Three

Routes into the Work-force

Old and new routes

In *Young Workers* (1976), a book based on studies of Leicester school-leavers, Ashton and Field argued that most school-leavers joined one of three broad career streams. The first group embarked on *extended careers*. These careers were usually launched from educational success. The young people typically stayed at school beyond 16 for A-levels and some entered higher education. On starting work they stepped onto the lower rungs of career ladders which they could ascend throughout their working lives as they gained experience, skill, and knowledge, sometimes complemented by formal post-entry education and qualifications. Central and local government offered such careers. So did banks and insurance companies, professions such as law, accountancy, medicine, and engineering, and businesses that recruited management trainees.

A second group embarked on *short careers*. Apprentices were the clearest examples. Entry to these occupations usually depended on a modicum of educational success. On entering apprenticeships young people received systematic training lasting several years which led to fully qualified skilled status. So in their early working lives the individuals experienced upward mobility. They moved from being trainees who could work only under supervision to become fully skilled and capable of training others. These individuals' careers were short because there was not the same distance in time, status, or pay between their starting and finishing points as in the extended careers. Individuals on short careers would become skilled by their early twenties after which they were unlikely to rise higher. By this age they would normally be achieving close to their peak earnings. Thereafter they could expect no regular career progression though promotion to supervisory and junior management posts was possible for individuals who displayed special talent and were in the right places at the right times.

However, after their short rises early in their working lives most of this group had to rely on piece rates or overtime to increase their earnings, or seize opportunities that arose to change jobs or employers into positions that were marginally more attractive.

Ashton and Field's third group was *careerless*. These individuals left school and entered jobs in which they could become fully productive, justifying their pay, within months, weeks or days in some cases. The young people who took such jobs mostly left education at the earliest opportunity without any qualifications and never returned even on a part-time basis. They took jobs in which there were no structured prospects of progression. Like the individuals who experienced short careers, any improvements in their terms and conditions of employment normally depended on moving to better, but typically still unskilled jobs as and when opportunities arose. Maximizing their earnings depended less on acquiring skills incrementally than working overtime, quickly on piece rates, at unsocial hours, or in jobs that were especially arduous or disagreeable in some other way.

Ashton and Field also argued that most young workers were fairly easily reconciled to their career opportunities on account of their anticipatory socialization. Those destined for extended careers usually had similar experiences in education; of passing examinations and progressing to higher level courses and qualifications. Such young people tended to be from families whose adult members had extended careers. Their experiences at home and school led the young people to expect comparable opportunities when they entered employment. Careerless young people, in contrast, had typically experienced repeated failure in education. They left school without qualifications having learnt that their abilities were limited and that they were unsuited to study. They were never led to expect anything other than ordinary jobs. These types of employment were manifestly within their abilities and most of the young people considered themselves well-suited to the jobs. Their parents typically worked in non-skilled occupations and their experiences neither at home nor at school led the young people to anticipate anything better. The organization of education and the occupational structure were sufficiently similar to equip most school-leavers with self-concepts and aspirations consistent with their futures. Thus the work-force could be reproduced from generation to generation while permitting a limited volume of social mobility.

Ashton and Field did not argue that the occupational structure was composed of just three kinds of jobs. In subsequent research David Ashton has drawn attention to how labour markets are intricately segmented by combinations of horizontal and vertical divisions (Ashton *et al.* 1989). His segmentation theory suggests that even when they change jobs individuals tend to remain in the same types of work. So when office staff change employment they are most likely to move into other offices jobs, sales staff into other sales jobs, and so on. This is the result of individuals gaining experience and skills that will be rewarded only while they remain within their labour market segments, and employers preferring recruits who have already proved that they can be satisfactory in similar jobs. Despite these complications, young people's career routes could still be grouped into the three basic types.

By the end of the 1980s young people's routes into the work-force had become more numerous and complicated. Much had changed. It was no longer just academic high-fliers who were remaining in full-time education beyond age 16. Instead of taking academic courses young people could opt for vocational programmes. Traditional apprenticeships had become scarcer. Meanwhile new forms of training had been introduced, some receiving government support under the successive versions of Youth Training. Some of these training provisions were employer based while others were based in training workshops and community organizations. From the mid-1970s onwards unemployment had been adding to the complexity of young people's transitions.

When new vocational courses and training schemes were introduced this was invariably amid claims that they would open new routes into skilled occupations, equip young people with the skills that the economy needed, and widen the horizons of the young people who would otherwise have been the most disadvantaged, namely, the careerless group in Ashton and Field's typology. This chapter assesses whether Britain's new routes through vocational education and Youth Training have achieved these stated objectives. In particular it asks whether the new provisions really have become new routes into skilled employment thereby making a difference to who gets these jobs. By the early 1990s the balance of evidence suggested that the new measures had failed abjectly in these respects. They had certainly complicated the entry into employment but beneath the surface basic structures and relationships remained intact. The evidence from the ESRC 16–19 Initiative suggested that up to the end of the 1980s Britain still had just two main routes to good jobs and that these were basically the same routes that had been identified in the 1970s and before—success in academic education, and being trained by an employer for a skilled job in the industry or business.

Vocational education

Outside the mainstream

Vocational or technical education in Britain has a heroic but rather sad history. It has never gained equivalent status to its counterparts in continental Europe. When Germany was founding technological universities in the late nineteenth and early twentieth centuries Britain was developing technical colleges which stood apart from the academic mainstream of secondary schools which fed into the universities. The technical colleges, together with their courses and qualifications, always had inferior status.

There have been numerous attempts to raise the status of technical education in Britain. When the 1944 Education Act was passed the intention was that there should be a tripartite system of grammar, technical, and secondary modern schools which would be different but equal. In the event the technical sector contracted instead of expanding. Many of the technical schools that had been developed before the Second World War subsequently transformed themselves into grammar schools. Meanwhile, allocation to secondary moderns, the schools which were intended to offer practical syllabuses, was regarded as failing the 11-plus. These schools were unpopular and by the end of the 1970s the majority had been replaced by comprehensives, in which most pupils were exposed to either full-blown or diluted versions of the academic grammar school curriculum.

In 1956 selected technical and further education colleges were upgraded into Colleges of Advanced Technology and a new qualification, the Diploma in Technology, was introduced to raise the profile and status of advanced technical studies. In the mid-1960s, following the Robbins Report (1963) on higher education, most of these institutions became new universities. The Robbins Committee urged this in order that the institutions, their courses and students should have equal status to mainstream higher education. Subsequently these institution's courses and students became indistinguishable from other universities'. From 1966 onwards a new generation of Polytechnics was created which were supposed to offer an alternative, more vocationally relevant form of higher education. In 1991 these institutions became yet another generation of new universities. The cycle of academic drift and absorption had been repeated.

In Germany and most other European countries technical secondary schools and higher education institutions have sufficient status to attract and retain pupils and students of average and better ability.

Technical education in Britain has never exerted comparable appeal. It has always hit cultural barriers. Academic education is long established and prestigious. Alternative types of education have never been able to match the appeal of academic courses and qualifications. According to one school of thought, the roots of this situation lie in Britain having become the first industrial nation which enabled the country to modernize without international competition forcing a cultural revolution (Weiner 1981). Manufacturing and applying knowledge have never earned recognition as élite talents in Britain. The country has therefore lacked the cultural foundations for high status vocational education. Vocational schools, colleges, courses, and qualifications have either undergone 'academic drift' and been absorbed into the academic mainstream, or they have been kept in education's second or third divisions. Employers have been part of this cultural fix. Their knee-jerk reaction may be to express approval of any new scheme or course with technical or vocational in the title, but when recruiting to high status jobs these same employers generally prefer applicants with academic credentials.

This book is not wholly dismissive, but it is consistently sceptical towards allegations that inadequate vocational preparation, including weaknesses in technical education, have retarded Britain's economic performance during the twentieth century. This case is regarded as not proven. Fence-sitting is excusable because the problem is not strictly sociological. The sociologically noteworthy points are that the diagnosis has been made repeatedly since the 1860s, governments have repeatedly tried to strengthen technical education, but today the diagnosis remains as plausible as ever even if still not fully proven. Attempts to raise the status and to strengthen and enlarge the role of vocational education have consistently underestimated the conservative force of existing educational structures and national culture. Have there been any good reasons to expect recent efforts to strengthen vocational education to be more successful than their predecessors?

NVQs

As explained in Chapter One, Britain's most recent vocational education drive began in the 1970s when youth unemployment rose, education came under critical scrutiny, and work experience for secondary pupils was recommended and implemented. The Technical and Vocational Education Initiative was launched in 1983. Subsequently, however, government policies have pinned their best hopes of success on a new set of qualifications, namely National Vocational Qualifications (NVQs) and their Scottish equivalents.

The first point to note about this strategy is that it is anything but novel. Using new qualifications to raise the profile and prestige of vocational studies began with the efforts of non-government examining bodies, most notably the City and Guilds of London Institute, and continued after the First World War with the government backed introduction of National Certificates and Diplomas available at ordinary and higher levels, then the Diploma in Technology in 1956, and the Business and Technology Education Council which absorbed the national certificates in the 1970s. NVQs, which were announced in 1986 and have subsequently become increasingly available, are supposed to succeed where their predecessors failed. Their success was intended to be facilitated if not guaranteed by placing employers in charge. The underlying reasoning has been that if the qualifications prove that their holders have the skills that employers want, the latter will use the qualifications in their recruitment, training, and promotion, and the qualifications will thereby become attractive to prospective students. The development of NVQs covering different industries has been under the auspices of employer dominated industrial lead bodies which specify the skills that students or trainees need to demonstrate to be awarded the qualifications at Levels 1 to 5. NVQs differ from most other qualifications in that they certify that an individual has acquired a vocational skill. The teaching and testing may be in a college, a place of work, or a training workshop. Detailed syllabuses and methods of instruction are not prescribed. Trainers and teachers can devise their own methods provided these lead to the acquisition of the relevant skills. Because they certify what an individual can do, and because these skills have been identified by employers as vocationally relevant, the expectation has been that employers will recognize and reward the qualifications.

NVQs are intended to be pursued after age 16, usually by individuals who are receiving employer-based training. However, there are also General National Vocational Qualifications (GNVQs), which certify skills common to a range of occupations and which can be obtained through full-time or part-time study, usually in further education but in some secondary schools also. GNVQs are available at Levels 1, 2, and 3, and the highest qualifications of this type have been described as vocational A-levels. The government has decreed that Level 3 NVQs are the A-level equivalent. However, these matters are never settled by government edict. Whether any qualification becomes an A-level or degree equivalent depends ultimately on the admissions policies of higher education institutions and employers' recruitment and promotion practices. The latter were always going to be crucial to the success of

NVQs. It was by the qualifications opening access to skilled jobs that this type of vocational education was to create new and attractive routes into the work-force, open to young people whose potential was not recognized on academic courses, thereby producing new answers to 'Who gets which jobs?'

By the early 1990s the evidence was not encouraging. It is necessary to make a distinction between the career significance of vocational qualifications obtained prior to and after entering employment. Vocational education in Britain was initially developed mainly for people in employment who were simultaneously being trained in their workplaces, whose employers encouraged them to study in the evenings or granted day release, and rewarded the students' efforts with pay increments and improved career prospects. At all levels, from the skilled manual trades to the highest status professions, specialized vocational education and qualifications have worked best as career boosters in Britain for people in employment. The same is likely to apply to NVQs, especially low level NVQs. By the early 1990s many firms had begun using these qualifications to enhance the status of the training given to their own staff but the same employers were far less likely to attach any weight to such qualifications gained in education or with other employers when individuals applied for jobs in the firms (Roberts and Corcoran-Nantes 1994). British employers tend to insist that their own skill requirements are firm specific. Vocational experience and qualifications gained elsewhere may be treated as evidence that an individual will be trainable if recruited, but not necessarily as proof that the person already possesses the competences that are required. The main exceptions to this are when individuals have completed full professional or apprentice training with another employer, but even then they are regarded as carrying the disadvantage of needing to 'learn the ropes' again when recruited by a new company.

Career returns

Bennett and his colleagues (1992*a* and 1992*b*) have studied the career returns that accrue to various types of qualifications in Britain. Career returns were measured in terms of pay and avoiding unemployment. Their conclusion was that the vocational returns on NVQs beneath Level 3 (the A-level equivalent) were usually nil. The main exceptions were when individuals were formerly completely unqualified. Young people who already possessed reasonable academic qualifications did not appear to derive any long-term career benefits from courses and training leading to NVQs at Levels 1 and 2. Bennett found that A-levels yielded better, though still modest returns. The big gains were from higher education.

A note of caution that must be attached to this evidence is that the findings could be outdated. It is never possible to measure the full career returns from any course or qualification until the individuals have completed their careers. Interim measurements may be satisfactory substitutes but it is still necessary to wait some years after qualifications have been obtained before measuring the returns or their absence. Since the 1970s Britain's vocational education and training have been subject to so many reforms and initiatives that there have always been doubts as to whether even the latest research findings still apply. In the short term the best way of judging the likely impact of any new initiatives is to use past evidence to identify the underlying processes that are likely to shape the performance of reforms of old, and new courses and qualifications. It is this kind of reasoning, as well as the harder evidence from the past, that leads to pessimism as regards the likely career gains from present-day vocational education.

Of course, there will always be exceptions. Some vocational qualifications have been extremely advantageous when seeking specific types of initial employment. Qualifications in clerical skills—typing for example—increase the holders' employability. For young people in general, however, the labour market signals created by employers' recruitment practices suggest that their best strategy will be to stay in the academic mainstream for as long as possible, preferably through higher education, rather than switch to vocational options. These are in fact the choices that young people have been making. As explained in Chapter One, there has been a big increase in the number of young people remaining in full-time education after age 16. The numbers on both academic and vocational courses have risen but it is the academic courses that have accounted for the majority of the new students. These courses have the greater prestige and normally yield the greater career returns. Table 8 describes the numbers of 16–18-year-olds in different kinds of full-time education, and the trends from 1979–80 to 1991–2. Throughout this period the most popular vocational qualifications sought by full-time students were BTECs. Most of the 'other' courses in Table 8 were also vocational and the number of students in this category should be added to the BTEC group when assessing the appeal of vocational courses. It is clear from Table 8, first, that in 1991–2 there were far more 16-, 17- and 18-year-olds on academic than on vocational courses, and that since 1979–80 the numbers in the age group seeking academic qualifications had grown more than the numbers on full-time vocational courses.

Table 8 Full-time education: 16–18-year-olds (England)

16-year-olds (in percentages) Full-time	1979–80	1985–6	1991–2
A/AS	20.8	21.7	34.9
BTEC National	1.9	3.7	8.9
GCSE	9.3	10.1	11.6
Other	9.3	11.3	11.2
	41.7	47.4	67.1
17-year-olds (in percentages)			
Higher	0.3	0.2	0.3
A/AS	18.7	20.1	31.4
BTEC National	1.5	3.7	8.1
GCSE	1.6	1.8	2.1
Other	4.8	5.8	6.7
	27.1	32.0	49.0
18-year-olds (in percentages)			
Higher	8.0	8.1	13.7
A/AS	3.2	3.9	6.1
BTEC National	0.8	1.9	4.3
GCSE	0.3	0.4	0.5
Other	2.3	2.6	3.7
	14.7	17.1	28.5

Students' attitudes

All the relevant surveys show that young people are anything but hostile to the idea of vocational education. When on their courses they are often enthusiastic. In secondary schools and further education many students prefer to learn skills of obvious practical value rather than abstract academic knowledge. Moreover, vocational courses can offer positive experiences of success to students who can learn skills and meet targets but whose performances in academic examinations—modest grade passes in GCSE for example—are generally regarded as failing. Teachers have found that students of average and below average academic ability are better motivated when given vocational options (Brown 1987).

It has rarely been difficult to recruit students to new vocational programmes. In 1986 a new Certificate of Pre-Vocational Education (CPVE) was launched—one-year full-time courses aimed at 16-year-olds without the academic records normally required to proceed to A-levels. The CPVE proved short-lived not because of students refusing to enrol but because the qualification never established credibility with employers. Lower level NVQs have encountered this problem. When new courses and qualifications are introduced they usually recruit initial waves of enthusiastic students but are then discredited when the qualifications fail to open access to good jobs. By the mid-1990s NVQs were being construed as certifying that their holders were 'not very qualified' throughout much of British industry.

The real labour market function of much low level full-time vocational education is 'warehousing'. The courses hold students in 'waiting rooms' or 'parking lots' until they are able to obtain jobs, but without improving the levels of employment at which they will be credible applicants. The courses may prevent students' work motivation deteriorating. Months or years spent as a student are certainly

---

THE SMITHERS REPORT

'. . . The National Council for Vocational Qualifications has departed from established educational practice. It has insisted that students should be assessed solely on what they can do rather than including also what they understand' (p. 9).

In 1993 Alan Smithers, Professor of Education at the University of Manchester, produced a highly critical report on NVQs for Channel 4 Television. His report was based on visits to centres where NVQs were taught, discussions with teachers and employers, and comparisons with practices in continental Europe.

The report concludes that Britain's new courses and qualifications are inferior to those offered by the older examining bodies. It argues that the changes are vocationally retrograde; that workers really need to understand 'the reasons why' rather than just 'how to do it' so that they will be able to improve and adapt to change. Rather than catching up or overtaking, the report argues that in terms of vocational education Britain is falling further behind the rest of Europe.

The report is particularly critical of how NVQ competences are tested by teachers and supervisors whose institutions may be paid only if the students pass. This is said to create pressures to blur standards and pass virtually everyone, and to stifle criticism from those who know what is going on.

A. Smithers, *All Our Futures: Britain's Educational Revolution*, Channel 4 Television, London, 1993.

---

preferable to a career history of prolonged unemployment when approaching prospective employers. But vocational students do not improve their career prospects to the same extent as their counterparts who remain in the academic mainstream.

Academic rejection

There are different ways of reacting to the Smithers Report (see p. 65). One might take the criticisms of NVQs at face value and conclude that they deserve to fail because their success would be economically and educationally damaging. Alternatively, the report might be read as a view from the academic establishment illustrating the ingrained distrust of anything which departs from customary academic practice— evaluating learning outcomes rather than processes, and practical skills rather than underlying knowledge, and paying by results, for example. However, in so far as Smithers' views are widely shared within education it is unlikely that NVQs will be treated as A-level equivalents, for university entry for example.

Educators, young people, and employers in Britain have learnt to know and trust traditional academic qualifications, and a result has been that vocational courses have always found it difficult to break in. This may or may not have been an economic handicap for Britain. It is not self-evident that custom and practice in Britain whereby education concentrates on imparting general knowledge and developing generic intellectual abilities, while vocational skills are learnt in employment, is economically unsound. However, the inability of vocational education to create routes into jobs of equivalent status to those associated with academic courses has led to stresses. Sixteen-year-olds struggle to remain in the academic mainstream, repeating GCSEs and taking one or two rather than the customary three or four A-levels, for example. It is doubtful whether such additions to their qualification portfolios have any significant labour market value. Many students fail or drop out, having found the courses inappropriate. Some sections of post-16 academic education in Britain seem to have taken on the *cooling-out function* of North America's junior colleges (Clark 1960). The stated purpose of the courses is to equip students with qualifications that will give them access to higher education or good jobs but their real latent function is to prove to the students that they lack the necessary ability and, in the process, to subdue their aspirations.

Access to higher education

The vast increase in the numbers of 16- and 17-year-olds in full-time education in Britain, mostly on academic courses, has not been matched by comparable growth in the proportion of the age group gaining three or more A-levels. Higher education has expanded not so much in response to a growth in the number of conventionally qualified applicants but by recruiting more with non-conventional entry qualifications, one or two A-levels or BTECs, and mature students.

Table 9 Destinations of students who completed BTEC National Diplomas in 1993 (%)

Higher education	57
Other full-time education	7
Employment	30
Unemployment	5

BTECs, which pre-date NVQs, have been Britain's main success story in vocational education in recent years, certainly in terms of the numbers of 16–18-year-olds who have been recruited on to full-time courses. However, this success has been associated with a pronounced academic drift, gaining recognition as an A-level equivalent within education. In 1993 roughly two-thirds of students who were awarded National Diplomas, usually following two years of full-time study, continued in education (see Table 9). Most of these entered higher education. BTECs' popularity derives from offering a route back into the academic mainstream rather than having become the prime entry qualification for status jobs in the industries and occupations to which the courses relate. This is even more true of lower level BTECs. In 1993 74 per cent of First Diploma completers continued in education, mostly heading towards National Diplomas.

Full-time vocational education has won a niche by shadowing mainstream academic courses, and this has been possible in recent years because additional higher education places have been created. However, the shortage of graduate jobs could lead to certain sections of higher education taking on the cooling-out and warehousing roles formerly associated with lower level academic and vocational education.

A 14-plus?

There are several ways in which policy makers could respond to Britain's 'mixed' track record in vocational education. One would be the Frank Sinatra response of, 'Let me try again', which would mean persisting with NVQs or a substitute if and when these qualifications lost credibility. Another would be to reform A-levels to make the courses suitable for more young people but there would be strong opposition to 'diluting the gold standard'. Another, currently favoured by the Labour Party, would be to subsume A-levels and vocational qualifications within a single framework which endowed them with equal status but this would not guarantee their equal treatment by employers or within education.

There is a more radical policy option which was considered and rejected in the early 1980s. When YTS was introduced in 1983, and TVEI began its pilot projects in that same year, there were suggestions that TVEI courses from age 14 might dovetail with YTS to create integrated vocational routes for a band of Britain's 14–18-year-olds. There was also the option of making YTS education based with trainees being sent out for work experience. In the event, however, YTS became mostly employer based with trainees sometimes attending colleges for off-the-job training. Rather than separate TVEI streams being created, this initiative was implemented so as to enrich the education of all or most pupils in the relevant schools. In the government's main reform of education in the 1980s, the 1988 Education Reform Act, a common curriculum for all 5–16-year-olds was prescribed. There was no division of pupils into separate academic and vocational tracks.

In 1994 the Department of Trade and Industry's White Paper on *Competitiveness* proposed changes that could lead to a clearer division between academic and vocational tracks from age 14; streamlining the national curriculum to focus on 'basics', a new General Diploma for (academic) students gaining five GCSE passes at grades A–C, and more opportunities (presumably for other pupils) to undertake vocational studies from age 14. However, the standard criticisms that are hurled at such ideas—reinventing the 11-plus, and separating pupils into the academic sheep and the vocational goats—indicate the problems that such a policy would encounter. The chances are that following any such division pupils with any hope of academic success, together with their parents, would demand the opportunity to attempt the academic route. The vocational track would then be saddled with the reputation of handling the academic failures. This, indeed, is a difficulty that has always stigmatized attempts to introduce a full-time vocational route within education in Britain. Whether the courses have been aimed at the under- or over-16s they have always been tainted with the reputation of recruiting mainly young people who have found the academic path too demanding.

It is difficult to identify any 'good jobs' in Britain for which young people can better improve their chances of entry by taking full-time vocational rather than academic courses. Academic qualifications are the best predictors of labour market success. Students may enrol on further education courses in clothing design with hopes of obtaining glamour jobs in the international fashion industry but the majority are destined for more modest careers in the 'rag trade' (Bates 1993*b*). Likewise 16–18-year-olds may study for hotel and catering qualifications with hopes of managing five star establishments but at the end of their courses the majority realize that their immediate prospects are on the reception desks or in restaurants or kitchens unless they continue into higher education (Riseborough 1993a).

Youth Training

High hopes

Youth Training has been the other main recent attempt to create new routes into the work-force. The Youth Training Scheme (YTS) was launched in 1983 with high aspirations though it was difficult to tell the extent to which politicians and scheme organizers were expressing their real expectations because, as has applied with all other initiatives, they knew that they needed to 'talk up' YTS to give the scheme any chance of success.

In 1983 the YTS was intended to be quite different from the Youth Opportunities Programme (YOP) that it replaced. YOP had normally offered six months' work experience to otherwise unemployed 16- and 17-year-olds. YTS was to be different. It was launched as Stage One in a New Training Initiative. It was intended to be a training scheme first and foremost rather than just another alternative to unemployment. The young people on the scheme could be trainees or employees. They were all to receive quality training which would last for up to twelve months, extended to two years in 1986. All trainees were to be able to gain a worthwhile qualification, initially meaning the YTS certificate but subsequently the 'worthwhile' qualifications were said to be any other qualifications listed on the YTS certificate itself. YTS was intended to create opportunities for young people who were not necessarily academically gifted to prove that they had vocational abilities and thereby qualify for good jobs. Equal opportunities were enshrined in the scheme's objectives. Girls and ethnic minorities were expected to derive special benefits. What went wrong?

The context of unemployment

First, the scheme was launched in a context of high unemployment. David Raffe (1987) has argued that whatever politicians and scheme organizers said, it was inevitable that young people would see the scheme primarily as an alternative to unemployment and that employers would view trainees as young people who had been unable to obtain proper jobs. This was indeed how school-leavers in the 1980s viewed YTS. They left school and searched for jobs, and considered schemes only if they were unable to obtain employment (Roberts *et al.* 1987).

Whatever the content of the training, the context in which YTS operated was probably always going to be a stronger influence on the scheme's character. Some of the early generations of trainees were critical of the quality of their training but this was not the most widespread criticism. The main complaint was that the training allowance was derisory. Trainees who were firm based often complained of being exploited, especially when their training involved doing jobs for which other workers were paid wages. However, many young people were prepared to tolerate this treatment. They took the view that such training was 'better than the dole', but this was among the scheme's problems. Despite the advertising which stressed that the scheme was about training, school-leavers who entered usually did so only because their sole alternative was unemployment.

A franchise scheme

Secondly, the scheme was subject to only weak central regulation. Employers and other scheme organizers were given considerable discretion in delivering the training. The government felt that it needed to make the scheme attractive to employers in order to ensure that sufficient training places were offered. Compared with German apprenticeships, Youth Training providers in Britain were given generous government subsidies and far more discretion (Raggatt 1988).

Chandler and Wallace (1990) have argued that German apprenticeships operate on corporatist lines. The training that must be given is prescribed in agreements between government bodies, employers associations, and trade unions. In contrast, they argue that Britain's

YTS developed as a franchise scheme. In exchange for complying with a minimal set of conditions such as the equivalent of thirteen weeks' off-the-job training in any year, training providers were eligible for subsidies and were able to use the YTS 'logo' on their own versions of youth training.

In the late 1980s and early 1990s central regulation of the scheme became even weaker when its administration was handed to local Training and Enterprise Councils (TECs) in England and Wales and Local Enterprise Councils (LECs) in Scotland (see below). Training providers then began to be paid by the government not according to the numbers who received agreed training (bums on seats) but according to outcomes measured in terms of NVQs and subsequent employment rates.

Types of YT

By the mid-1980s it was clear that employers were using their discretion to run YTS in quite different ways. Some were using the scheme to subsidize their own longer programmes of training. Others were operating 'youth try-out schemes' in which they were able to assess young people over twelve months then retain the best and discard the rest. Others were creating temporary low grade jobs (Roberts *et al.* 1986).

SCOTTISH YOUNG PEOPLE'S SURVEYS

These inquiries began in 1976 as biennial surveys of national samples of school-leavers. During the 1980s the surveys became more longitudinal in recognition that transitions into employment had been prolonged. This series of investigations is now the UK's best source of evidence on how young people's transitions have changed over time. The England and Wales Youth Cohort Surveys (see page 24) commenced later, in 1985.

The Scottish Young People's Surveys have been used to explore whose careers have been affected, and how, as new education and training provisions have been introduced.

Some articles arising from this research are in D. Raffe (ed.), *Education and the Youth Labour Market* (Falmer Press, Lewes, 1988).

A. Furlong, *Growing Up in a Classless Society?* (Edinburgh University Press, Edinburgh, 1992), uses evidence from different cohorts to present an overview of how transitions in Scotland changed during the 1980s.

David Raffe (1988) has used evidence from the Scottish Young People's Surveys to construct a typology of training schemes. This typology identifies four sectors. The first is called the *sponsorship sector*, where trainees are given progressive training, which equips them for longer-term careers in the firms where their training took place. The second group of schemes is called a *contest sector*. These are schemes which employers use to sift entrants thereby placing trainees in competition with one another for a limited number of proper jobs. The third sector is described as *credentialling*. These are schemes where there are poor or zero prospects of the young people being retained by the companies where they are trained but which enable the trainees to gain qualifications which strengthen their chances in external labour markets. The fourth sector is labelled *detached* and is composed of schemes which offer none of the advantages found in the other sectors. These sectors were first identified by David Raffe and the labels have subsequently been used by other academic writers but, needless to say, never by the Employment Department in its official descriptions of Youth Training.

Other research has broadly confirmed Raffe's typology. The findings from the Scottish Young People's Surveys and the ESRC 16–19 Initiative show that in both England and Scotland most of the young people who benefited from Youth Training did so as a result of being retained in the firms where they were trained. Both sets of inquiries have emphasized how few trainees found that experience and qualifications gained on the scheme were any advantage when taken into wider labour markets. The credentialling sector was tiny. Trainees who were not kept on carried the stigma of having been discarded. The ESRC 16–19 Initiative also confirmed the existence of a substantial detached or 'warehousing' sector in which young people were 'parked' without gaining any long-term career benefits from their training (Roberts and Parsell 1992*a*).

The Southwich study confirmed the existence of a hierarchy of schemes. It also revealed how the divisions between different sectors were widening and hardening over time. This was occurring as schemes acquired particular reputations among school-leavers, teachers, and employers, and as tighter government funding pressured scheme organizers into concentrating on what they were able to do most cost effectively. In some cases this meant restricting quality training to quality entrants whom the firms expected to retain. In other cases it meant using trainees as cheap and temporary labour.

THE SOUTHWICH STUDY

Between 1983 and 1988 David Lee and his colleagues at the University of Essex conducted a detailed study of young people's progress through Youth Training and the development of schemes in the economically buoyant southern England town of 'Southwich'. They interviewed over 200 young people who entered YTS in 1984 and the majority were interviewed again in 1986 when they were aged up to 20.

This research also involved interviews with teachers, employers, and training staff who were responsible for delivering Youth Training.

This inquiry has several special features. First, it was able to relate the operation of training schemes to their local educational and labour market contexts. Secondly, it followed young people from entering Youth Training into their subsequent working lives. Thirdly, the research continued over a sufficiently long period to reveal how schemes were changing during the 1980s.

D. J. Lee *et al.*, *Scheming for Youth: A Study of YTS in the Enterprise Culture* (Open University Press, Milton Keynes, 1989).

Equal opportunities?

The Southwich study also drew attention to how entry to different kinds of schemes quickly became governed by young people's secondary school attainments and the particular schools that they had attended, their family backgrounds, and their sex. Good schemes, those in the sponsorship sector, were able to pick and choose and restrict entry to reasonably qualified school-leavers. Despite any aspirations to equal opportunities, training schemes became gender divided. Boys were trained for masculine jobs and girls for women's work (see Cockburn 1987). There was stronger gender segmentation within Youth Training than among young people in academic education. Girls have been more likely to break into male occupations through academic success than via Youth Training. Recent experience across Europe shows that existing gender divisions in employment tend to extend downwards into training schemes and vocational courses. Academic syllabuses have by far the best track records in challenging existing gender divisions (Buchmann and Charles 1992).

Research in several parts of Britain has found that school-leavers from different ethnic groups have tended to be channelled into different kinds of training schemes. Basically, black young people have been concentrated on the schemes with the poorest employment prospects (Connolly *et al.* 1991; Cross and Smith 1987).

By the late 1980s Youth Training was clearly experiencing the same problems as the earlier Youth Opportunities Programme. When special measures were first introduced in the 1970s the employment prospects of the otherwise disadvantaged young people who entered seemed to benefit. Subsequently, as YOP was enlarged and more young people were recruited, the Programme's overall success rate (measured in terms of progression into jobs) declined, and the advantages and disadvantages with which young people entered the Programme by virtue of their secondary school attainments, for example, were carried into their subsequent working lives (Greaves 1983). In social life it is always dangerous to assume that the results of experimental innovations will be sustained if the measures are implemented on a wider scale. It becomes more difficult to enlarge the career opportunities of girls, working-class young people, and ethnic minorities when the scale of the changes would make a significant difference to the prospects of other groups. By the late 1980s Youth Training was not so much challenging and changing as reproducing advantages and disadvantages.

The disintegration of Youth Training

In the late 1980s and early 1990s Youth Training was caught in a triple squeeze. The downward demographic trend was reducing the size of school-leaving cohorts. Retention rates in education were rising. Simultaneously, economic recession took hold and unemployment rose. The numbers on Youth Training declined (see Figure 4), as did the proportions of trainees gaining qualifications and progressing into employment (see Figure 5). However, the proportion of trainees with employee status also rose (see Table 10). The indications were that Youth Training was becoming an even more stratified set of schemes. On the one hand, some firms continued to use the scheme to support the initial stages in their employees' training. Other schemes were increasingly warehousing young people who did not wish to remain in education but were unable to find employment. While on Youth Training only a minority of these young people gained any qualifications, and many left and then became unemployed once more.

Rather than announce failure and cull Youth Training abruptly, the Employment Department appeared to opt for letting the scheme disappear slowly. In 1990 the administration of the scheme, along with other Employment Department measures, was handed to the TECs and

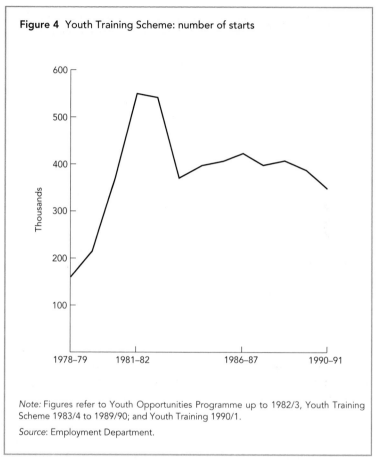

Figure 4 Youth Training Scheme: number of starts

Note: Figures refer to Youth Opportunities Programme up to 1982/3, Youth Training Scheme 1983/4 to 1989/90; and Youth Training 1990/1.

Source: Employment Department.

LECs. Members of these Councils were appointed by the Employment Department and the majority were employers. In the 1970s 'community involvement' in Employment Department measures had been encouraged. By the 1990s this was being replaced by employer control. With the change in administration the word 'Scheme' was dropped from the title of Youth Training. The TECs and LECs were expected to make the implementation of Employment Department programmes responsive to local needs. In practice this was bound to mean responsive to employers' wishes. One result, according to Frank Coffield (1992), was more low quality training geared to firms' short-term labour

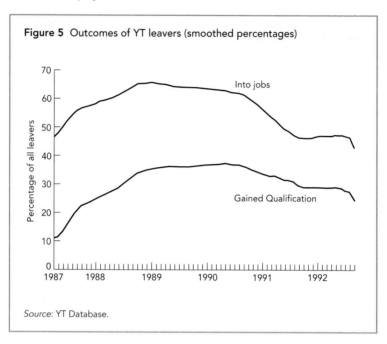

Figure 5 Outcomes of YT leavers (smoothed percentages)

Source: YT Database.

requirements. In the early 1990s the payment of Employment Department subsidies via the TECs and LECs was made more dependent on training outcomes. A consequence was to strengthen training deliverers' preference for 'trainable' school-leavers and there was evidence (see Chapter Four) of the least advantaged young people for

Table 10 Trainee status on last day of training (%)

	Employed	Non-employed	Don't know/no answer
1986/7	3.6	96.4	—
1987/8	6.3	93.7	—
1988/9	14.3	85.7	—
1989/90	21.8	78.2	—
1990/1	36.0	55.1	8.9
1991/2	33.7	57.7	8.6

Source: YT Management Information.

whom special measures were originally designed being squeezed out altogether.

In 1991 the Employment Department began to pilot Training Credits or Youth Credits. As these were introduced the title Youth Training was dropped. Training Credits were distributed by TECs and LECs. Young people received vouchers and with or without any paper changing hands were given an entitlement to purchase training up to a specified, but not rigidly enforced, value. The restriction was that the credits could only be spent on approved training. An aim of Training Credits was to increase young people's sense of responsibility for their own training. Another was to increase the flexibility of government support. The value of credits could be tailored (by the TECs and LECs) so as to balance the supply and demand for training in particular local labour markets, and to increase trainers' willingness to recruit young people with whom 'positive outcomes' were least likely. Research by the Employment Department (1992) found that most employers and young people had positive views about Training Credits though neither party's labour market behaviour seemed to change. Independent research led to more critical conclusions, namely, that the ability to 'purchase' their own training could not improve young people's labour market prospects in the absence of parallel measures to improve the supply of training so that young people would be able to make real choices between provisions with attractive prospects (Felstead 1993; MacDonald and Coffield 1993).

Working against the grain

There are many possible reasons for the failure of Britain's recent innovations in training and vocational education to open new routes to good jobs. The economic environment could have been more hospitable. Youth unemployment has been a nationwide problem in most years since the mid-1970s and any initiatives would have been unable to guarantee any jobs, let alone good jobs, for everyone who stayed the courses. Inadequate funding is the explanation favoured by many who work in education and training. Given more money to boost the quality, maybe better results would have followed. Would they? Sociological analysis shows that the innovations have faced more fundamental problems. They have needed to battle against entrenched educational structures and employers' preferences and prejudices, all rooted in national history and culture.

In Britain 'real training' has always been provided in employment, and firms have usually trained for their own requirements and rarely in excess. Firms with reputations for quality training have always been vulnerable to 'poachers', but when recruiting from external labour markets few employers, and certainly not the quality trainers, have set much store by lower level vocational qualifications or work experience in other companies except, sometimes, as signals of personal qualities such as stability, career commitment, and an ability to acquire the kinds of skills that the recruiter is seeking. The respected entry qualifications, especially when recruiting beginners, have remained the familiar academic varieties.

Despite all the innovations of the 1970s and 80s there are still just two main routes into good jobs in present-day Britain. These routes are not alternatives but are normally followed consecutively. One is through academic education. It makes sense in career terms for young people to progress through mainstream academic education for as long as they are able, and preferably into higher education. The second route, usually followed after some degree of educational success, is to find a job in which training is offered and from which there are prospects of career progression within and maybe outside the company also. There is no evidence that Britain's young people have been reluctant to enter such jobs or to accept training when in them. In contrast, it is now known from experience in most households that training without jobs does not usually pay off.

There are no obvious reasons why Britain's main routes into the work-force, with young people developing general knowledge and abilities in academic education then being trained for specific jobs by their employers, should be incapable of meeting the economy's technical skill requirements. If Britain does too little quality training to produce a world class work-force this is most likely to be because it has too few world class firms and its actual enterprises have little need for world class labour. In an economy where training is normally employment led it is unlikely to be training deficiencies that hold firms back by restricting the supply of quality labour.

Britain's main routes into the work-force have continued to work well enough for many young people, and for most employers. Their architects have introduced the new measures for other people's children. Transitions into the work-force have been difficult for many young people since the 1970s not because Britain's transitional arrangements are basically flawed but because of weaknesses in the surrounding economy. These have led not just to persistent youth unemployment but side-effects such as young people remaining in academic education for longer than they are able to progress, and others entering training and vocational courses whose principal function is to offer temporary relief from joblessness. It should not be a cause for surprise if students' and trainees' motivation and compliance when on these schemes and courses have often been less than their teachers and trainers would have preferred.

Persistent inequalities

During the last thirty years some former long-standing inequalities in compulsory education have narrowed or, in some cases, been overturned. Girls now outperform boys (see Chapter Two). Social class differences have diminished. Comprehensive secondary schooling has blurred the links between types of education and social origins and destinations. Higher pass rates in a common GCSE examination and higher stay-on rates have meant that fewer working-class children fail at or before age 16. Working-class pupils have derived the greatest benefit from the all-round improvement in educational standards. They had the most to gain. Most children from middle-class homes were already gaining good O-levels and staying on (see McPherson and Willms 1987).

Table 11 Career experiences, 16–19

	Family background	
	Middle class %	Working class %
Continuous success	68	35
Mixed	30	54
Repeated failure	2	11

Source: Roberts and Parsell (1992).

However, beyond age 16 the familiar inequalities have been recreated. Most boys and girls are channelled into gender appropriate vocational education and training, then into gendered occupations. Simultaneously, as new hurdles have been created along most young people's routes towards employment the tendency has been for those from middle-class homes to succeed at successive stages while those from working-class families suffer setbacks. This has been demonstrated in the Scottish Young People's Surveys (see Furlong 1992) and in the ESRC 16–19 Initiative (see Roberts and Parsell 1992*b*). In the latter study middle-class young people were typically achieving above average qualifications at age 16, then proceeding to further full-time academic education, jobs with training, or training schemes in which they were trained by employers, and the majority subsequently entered higher education or skilled jobs. In other words, most young people from middle-class homes crossed all the hurdles without stumbling (see Table 11). Despite all the changes since the 1970s, their routes to adulthood had remained much the same. They were progressing through academic education on courses which had expanded, then into levels of employment where there were more jobs than formerly (see Chapter Two). It was working-class young people whose progress into the labour market had been most affected by the decline of youth employment and the creation of new forms of vocational education and training. Their performances during compulsory education may have improved substantially, but on average they still do less well in GCSEs than their middle-class contemporaries. Moreover, even when they are equally successful up to age 16 young people from working-class families are less likely to remain in the academic mainstream or progress into good jobs or training with prospects. And even if they succeed at these stages they are less likely to make the next transitions successfully and progress into higher education, or enter and hold on to skilled employment. Continuous success is the normal experience from age 16 to 20 for young people from middle-class backgrounds whereas among those from working-class homes the majority either experience repeated failure or have chequered careers (see Roberts and Parsell 1992*b*). It is impossible to draw final conclusions about rates of social mobility until a birth cohort has progressed well into adulthood. However, the probability is that after all the changes in young people's education, training, and employment opportunities since the 1960s, links between social origins and destinations will have remained much as before.

Sociologists have competing explanations for this 'constant flux'. One is that whatever the economic and educational contexts in modern societies, privileged families find ways to transmit their advantages and prevent their children's descent (Erikson and Goldthorpe 1992). So after age 16 young people from middle-class homes continue to benefit from their parents' financial support, social connections, encouragement to remain in the academic mainstream and insistence that they accept only good jobs. An alternative explanation is in terms of meritocracy (Saunders 1994). This explanation alleges that rates of social mobility in Britain have been, and remain, much as one would expect given the unequal distribution of ability among children from different social levels. Amid the economic and educational changes, this explanation maintains that 'the cream' still rises to the top while others fall behind. Arbitrating between these explanations is fortunately beyond the scope of this particular book.

The most encouraging trend since the 1970s for those seeking equal opportunities for young people from different social groups is probably in Britain's ethnic mosaic. In 1994 the University of Central England analysed its student population and was startled to discover that the only under-represented ethnic group compared with the UK population as a whole was those describing themselves as 'white'. All other ethnic groups were considerably over-represented (*Careers Guidance Today*, 2/2 (1994), 7). However, it has become less sensible than in the 1960s to generalize about Britain's non-white minorities and more necessary to recognize that there are numerous minority groups (Jones 1993). Britain's 'Asian' minorities are experiencing collective upward social mobility. On average pupils from 'Asian' families outperform the white population in education. Many young people from these groups have been progressing through higher education then into professional and management occupations. The 'Asian' section of the population also has an above average rate of self-employment and some families have achieved upward mobility as a result of their success in business. Meanwhile, notwithstanding the situation at the University of Central England, children from Afro-Caribbean backgrounds continue to underachieve in education compared with the white population (Swann Report 1985). Beyond age 16 they tend to enter the training schemes and courses with the poorest prospects and they have exceptionally high rates of unemployment (Clough and Drew 1985; Connolly *et al.* 1991).

Further reading

For critical, but constructive commentaries on the new opportunities that young people have been offered in vocational education and training see P. Brown (1987), *Schooling Ordinary Kids: Inequality, Unemployment and the New Vocationalism*, Tavistock, London; D. Finn (1987), *Training Without Jobs*, Macmillan, London; D. Gleeson (ed.), *Training and Its Alternatives*, Open University Press, Milton Keynes, 1990; M. Holt (ed.) (1987), *Skills and Vocationalism: the Easy Answer*, Open University Press, Milton Keynes; and D. J. Lee, D. Marsden, P. Rickman and J. Duncombe (1989), *Scheming for Youth: a Study of YTS in the Enterprise Culture*, Open University Press, Milton Keynes.

Chapter Four

Learning to Labour in the 1990s

How things were: the conventional view

Chapter Three opened by describing three career types—extended, short, and careerless—that Ashton and Field (1976) identified in *Young Workers*. Their 1976 account of transitions into employment also contained a theory of occupational socialization. They argued that most school-leavers settled into employment with little difficulty because of continuities in their socialization in their homes, in education, then in employment. Young people from working-class homes knew that work would be work. Only those from middle-class families grew up expecting their initial jobs to lead to long careers. From their levels of success at school young people were able to anticipate the levels at which they would enter the labour market, so the majority were able to start work without any acute culture shock. Ashton and Field acknowledged that socially mobile young people could experience problems. They recognized that the downwardly mobile might flounder but argued that the upwardly mobile would be motivated to overcome any difficulties.

Research in the 1950s, 60s, and 70s did not find most school-leavers entering the particular jobs that they said they wanted prior to leaving school, but few suffered acute disappointment; their choices were typically unstable. Some young people only formulated 'first choices' when requested to do so in careers interviews. On leaving school the majority did not immediately enter the jobs that they had long hoped for, but they were able to obtain employment at the levels that they had anticipated. Subsequently the majority focused their ambitions on the occupations that they had actually entered. This was partly through *cognitive dissonance*, a tendency to forget or deny that alternatives were ever desired or even possible. The ideology of choice which surrounded work entry discouraged individuals from expressing dissatisfaction with jobs that they themselves were deemed to have chosen. And once in employment they were subject to occupational socialization. Typically they would take pride in whatever skills they acquired, when interacting with colleagues they would learn beliefs about the importance of their occupations, and they would also to learn to value the particular rewards that their jobs offered—good pay, security, interesting work, service to the community, or whatever. Such processes of occupational socialization were noted among trainee doctors (Merton *et al.* 1957), and student physiologists and mechanical engineers (Becker and Carper 1956*a*, 1956*b*, 1957). These are high status occupations but very similar processes were also noted among printing apprentices (Flude and Whiteside 1971), apprentice construction electricians, business machine operators, and barbers (Geer 1972). These occupations are at least partly skilled. What about the young people who entered unskilled jobs? They seemed to become less attached to their occupations and had the highest rates of job changing. But even among these young people there was little overt dissatisfaction with their types of employment.

Unskilled youth had the highest rates of job mobility but job changing was fairly common at all occupational levels. Most young people did not stay for life, or even for long, in the jobs where they were initially socialized. However, as noted in Chapter Three, there has been a strong tendency for individuals to move within labour market *segments*, that is, between similar kinds of employment, thus minimizing adjustment problems.

Criticisms of the conventional view

School-leavers' worries

The conventional view of young people's occupational socialization, as described above, has been criticized in several ways and thereby subjected to a series of qualifications. First, it has been argued that the conventional view has understated young people's difficulties on entering the labour market. Ashton's account, and those of other writers who portrayed young people as moving along synchronized routes through education into corresponding levels of employment which moulded their expectations and aspirations in line with their destinies, have been accused of overlooking school-leavers' anxieties.

Hill and Scharff's (1976) interviews and group discussions in three secondary schools found that their future entry into employment was a source of worry for the majority; they had no prior assurances that they

---

LABOUR MARKET SEGMENTS

During the 1980s David Ashton and his colleagues at Leicester University applied a theory of labour market segmentation in their research in Leicester, St Albans, and Sunderland. In 1978 they conducted interviews with 350 employers and four years later they studied 1,786 18–24 year-olds.

These enquiries emphasized the extent to which levels and types of employment, and therefore school-leavers' opportunities, varied from place to place (see p. 40). The research also highlighted the extent to which local labour markets were segmented.

Segments are defined by horizontal and vertical divisions. Ashton and his colleagues found that some segments were closed to young people because alcohol or driving were involved, or the work was considered too responsible. Identifying labour market segments helped to explain why youth employment had declined sharply. Young people's job prospects had been affected adversely by the decline of industries such as textiles, hosiery, and footwear in which substantial numbers had once worked. Female school-leavers' job opportunities had also declined as the occupations in some segments where they had previously been employed—retailing, and hotels and catering—were split into part-time jobs (see pp. 57–8).

School-leavers' qualifications were found to exert most of their influence over the labour market segments that young people initially entered. Thereafter their qualifications had little bearing on their progress. Job changing was mainly within the segments that individuals had already entered.

The findings from this research are in D. N. Ashton, M. J. Maguire, and V. Garland, *Youth in the Labour Market*, Department of Employment Research Paper 34 (London, 1982), and D. N. Ashton and M. J. Maguire, *Young Adults in the Labour Market*, Department of Employment Research Paper 55 (London, 1986). The subsequent book, D. N. Ashton, M. J. Maguire, and M. Spillsbury, *Restructuring the Labour Market: The Implications for Youth* (Macmillan, London, 1989), is based partly on the findings from the earlier research.

---

would obtain jobs compatible with their ambitions or that they would find it easy to slot in. Furlong (1992) has also argued that young people have always worried about their labour market prospects. Fear of the labour market pre-dates the spread of youth unemployment in the 1970s.

Notwithstanding these criticisms, the conventional view seems to have been basically correct in so far as most young people adjusted very quickly once they entered employment. Whatever their fears and worries prior to school-leaving, the transition was neither a chronic nor prolonged source of stress for the majority.

Employers' problems

Some employers would say that if the majority of school-leavers ever made smooth transitions into the work-force this was possible only because their employers suffered in silence. Since the 1970s there has been a barrage of complaints about young people's attitudes and basic employability. Employers have been far less likely to complain about school-leavers lacking specific vocational skills. They have never expected young people to enter the labour market ready trained. Rather, employers have expected education to develop young people's general abilities after which they, the employers, have been willing to take over and train young people in particular jobs. Employers have felt able to train young people in the technicalities of work but less able to change attitudes. Young people, certainly too many of them, have been said to possess the 'wrong' attitudes towards authority, meaning that they are disrespectful and unwilling to do as they are told. Many are said to have unrealistic expectations about the pace at which their careers should progress and the pay to which they are entitled. Another common complaint has been that young people are unstable—that their attendance and timekeeping are poor and that they change jobs too readily. Young people are said to be unprepared to knuckle down and accept the routine of much employment. Child-centred education and permissive parents are sometimes held responsible.

In addition to 'qualifications', employers invariably stress that they want 'personal qualities'. Qualifications are considered most important for higher level jobs (Keil *et al.* 1982; Dench 1993). When filling lower level office and manual vacancies employers usually insist that it is less important for recruits to be educationally qualified than that they should be 'right types' (Hunt and Small 1981; Dench 1993). Employers want recruits who will be socially acceptable in the businesses, meaning non-troublesome, as well as technically suitable (Jenkins 1982).

Schools and further education have come under pressure to teach the 'social and life skills' that employers expect and which, therefore, young people are deemed to require. Some teachers have been keen to impart, and many students have been eager to acquire any skills that will give them an edge in the competition for jobs (Brown 1987). In contrast, many educationalists (people who study and write about education) have deplored the trend towards educating passive conformists rather than the critical individuals that liberal education has aimed to nurture (Holt 1987).

Employers try to ensure that recruits will be acceptable not by teaching social skills but by sifting out the unacceptable. Selection interviews are invariably part of the recruitment process and can be used to judge personal qualities. Large firms with personnel departments often use psychological tests. In practice most employers operate a number of filters. Some judge young (and adult) applicants in terms of group stereotypes. So individuals from particular schools, neighbourhoods, or ethnic groups may be deemed poor risks (Livock 1983). Another filter is recruitment via training schemes and temporary grades (Manwaring 1982).

A further method is to rely on informal recruitment channels—word of mouth recommendations. There was evidence in the 1980s of employers making greater use of informal recruitment (Manwaring 1982). These methods have several advantages for employers. They are inexpensive, managers can be given discretion to act according to the needs of their particular departments and work groups, and mistakes do not affect the entire companies. Employers often feel able to trust existing staff's recommendations. A person who has been a satisfactory employee is considered likely to recommend a similar type. The existing employee will not wish to tarnish his or her reputation by recommending someone unsuitable. And the newcomer is likely to feel obligated to the friend or relative who helped to obtain the job which will be another incentive to be non-troublesome (Keil *et al.* 1982). The extent to which employers trust informal recommendations is the reason why 'contacts' can be so important in determining who gets a job. Knowing people who are already in good jobs is a definite asset. One hears about jobs to apply for before any adverts are placed, and a friend's or relative's support can be decisive in surviving the various stages in recruitment.

A point that needs to be made about the debate on school-leavers' employability is that far less was heard about this problem prior to youth unemployment becoming a nationwide issue in the 1970s. When many employers had little option but to take whoever applied they seemed to accept the situation as a fact of life in a market economy. Like school-leavers' fears, employers' problems seem to be the type with which they can cope when necessary. It is only since the labour market balance tilted in employers' favour that they have felt able to act upon and broadcast their preferences for the 'right types'. Perhaps, however, it would be fairer to say that it is only since unemployment threatened school-leavers that teachers, young people, and researchers have seen reason to heed employers' problems and preferences.

Working-class resistance

A third criticism of the conventional view of school-leavers acquiring aspirations broadly consistent with the jobs they could enter, then being socialized into occupational cultures, is that the theory ignores all the evidence of working-class 'resistance'. It has been argued that the theory fails to take account of fundamental social class differences in young people's orientations towards education, employment and authority in general.

P. WILLIS, *LEARNING TO LABOUR* (Saxon House, Farnborough, 1977).

This book is a classic. It is based on qualitative, ethnographic research among young people who attended a secondary modern school in 'Hammertown', a West Midlands nuts and bolts town which had once been a cradle of Britain's industrial revolution. In his fieldwork Willis focused on twelve male pupils and retained contact with them during the first year of their working lives.

The book's influence has been a product of the quality of the fieldwork and Willis's analysis of his findings rather than the scale of the inquiry or the representativeness of the sample. The fieldwork was conducted when Willis was based at Birmingham University's Centre for Contemporary Cultural Studies. It was one of several research projects conducted at the Centre in the 1970s which challenged much that had previously been written about working-class young people. The work of the Centre at that time was influenced by Marxism. All its work made social class a central concept but focused on the cultural aspects of class (people's beliefs and values) as well as economic determinants.

One criticism of much of the Centre's work among young people in the 1970s, including Willis's study, is that girls were ignored or marginalized.

The secondary modern that Paul Willis studied was not a 'problem school'. Quite the reverse: it had a local reputation for its high standards and committed staff. Careers teaching was treated as an important and serious business. Nevertheless, 'the lads' whom Willis studied were immersed in a counter-school culture. Their entrenched opposition to authority and caged resentment stopped only just short of outright confrontation with their teachers. In their dress, smoking, and general demeanour the lads expressed their defiance daily. They were contemptuous of school knowledge and of passive 'ear 'oles'—pupils who were always listening (to the teachers) and never doing. The lads valued self-direction, laughs, and excitement. Rather than succeeding in education they felt that it was important to be one of the lads and to be seen to be so.

Previous researchers had drawn attention to school counter-cultures, typically involving males in secondary schools' non-academic streams. Prior to Willis's study these counter-cultures had been explained as a male reaction to the young people's treatment in education. Pupils who were rejected and denied status by their schools were said to respond by not just rejecting but inverting the schools' values. Willis, however, argued that his lads' culture drew upon broader working-class and shop floor cultures to which the young people were introduced in their homes and neighbourhoods. Their male chauvinism, contempt for the idiocy of theoretical knowledge, and the value they placed on informally wrestling control from authorities, were all features of Hammertown's broader working-class heritage.

The lads knew that their own culture was the best guide to their futures. They realised that they would not get good jobs. In any case, they did not want 'sissy jobs' but wanted to be real men doing real work and they knew that they did not need qualifications to obtain such employment. They also knew that work would be work and that which particular job hardly mattered. The lads' culture, therefore, was leading them to 'reject, ignore, invert, make fun of or transform most of what they [were] given in careers lessons' (p. 92).

Willis argued that his lads were not being passively channelled into jobs. Rather, they were actively choosing their own futures in unskilled work—'applauding their own damnation'. *Learning to Labour* highlights the paradox that the lads' resistance was a key process in reproducing the work-force. The lads' own choices propelled them into adulthoods in which they then had no choice but to continue to labour in unskilled jobs. Cultural practices which could be correctly construed as resistance in school situations were simultaneously forms of accommodation to working-class futures. Willis did not disagree with the conventional view that young people's prior experience in their families and education gave them access to the kinds of jobs that they were prepared to accept. However, he insisted that the processes whereby working-class young people ended up in working-class jobs were more complicated than previous writers had suggested, and also more 'problematic', meaning that the reproduction of the labour force was not to be regarded as inevitable and automatic. Rather, Willis argued that his lads' ability and willingness to resist indicated at least a partial awareness of their membership of an oppressed class. Hence the possibility of radical cultural and political work with such young people fostering the kind of class consciousness which would refuse to submit to capitalism's requirements.

Criticisms of resistance theory

All the main challenges to Willis's theory have queried who his lads represented apart from themselves. The subtitle of *Learning to Labour* is, 'How working-class kids get working-class jobs'. Although Willis did not claim that his lads were representative, the findings are presented as if they spoke for the entire working-class.

This has been disputed. On the basis of research in two South Wales comprehensive schools Phil Brown (1987) has argued that it is misleading to juxtapose pro- and counter-school cultures and to imagine that all or even most young people belong to one or the other. Most of the pupils at Brown's schools described themselves as 'ordinary kids'. They worked reasonably hard at school, expected to leave with some qualifications, and hoped for decent jobs. They were neither academically committed nor anti-school.

Furlong (1992) has made similar criticisms backed by evidence from the Scottish Young People's Surveys (see page 71). Furlong challenges the view that the majority of working-class school-leavers have ever been eager to enter unskilled jobs. For as long as the Scottish surveys have been conducted most working-class school-leavers have been moderately ambitious. Boys have hoped for apprenticeships and many girls have been keen to work in offices rather than shops or factories. It is unlikely that such working-class aspirations are recent novelties. Working-class fathers have a long history of instructing their sons on the virtues of learning a trade.

Willis can also be criticized for portraying middle-class young people, by implication, as passive conformists. They appear in his book mainly through the eyes of 'the lads'. Sixth-form and university students are known to have been involved in various counter cultures involving drug use and political protest. Some have resisted recruitment into boring careers in dull bureaucracies. Maybe young people from all social levels combine elements of conformity and resistance.

Another criticism is that girls were ignored in Willis's research or, like the ear 'oles, glimpsed only through the lads' eyes. Subsequently researchers have investigated the ways in which girls can resist. Christine Griffin (1985) attempted a near-replica of Willis's study with a sample of Birmingham girls. However, by the time that Griffin's research was under-way it had become more difficult for working-class 16-year-olds to celebrate their release from school by entering employment and earning decent wages. Unemployment had become a major threat. Transitions from school to schemes were replacing fast track transitions into employment. These new labour market conditions have called into question whether any of the conclusions about occupational socialization in the 1970s and before retain any relevance.

Youth unemployment

Since the 1970s youth unemployment has been a normal experience in most parts of the UK. It has been the number one issue in research among school-leavers. In fact unemployment is the reason why there has been so much research among youth in the labour market since the 1970s compared with the previous twenty years. The phrases coined during this research—new social condition, limbo, lost generation, broken bridges—stress the discontinuities with the preceding era. Yet we have seen that the main routes to good jobs, and who gets them, have survived the changes. Could the same apply to occupational socialization?

Table 12 Unemployment rates:[1] by sex and age United Kingdom (%)

	1984	1986	1988	1989	1990
Males					
16–19	23	22	15	12	13
20–9	16	16	11	9	9
30–9	9	9	7	6	6
40–9	8	8	6	5	4
50–9	9	9	9	7	7
60 and over	10	10	9	9	8
All males aged 16 and over	12	12	9	7	7
Females					
16–19	21	20	12	9	10
20–9	16	14	11	9	8
30–9	11	10	9	7	6
40–9	7	7	5	5	5
50–9	7	6	6	6	5
60 and over	7	5	5	5	4
All females aged 16 and over	12	11	8	7	6

[1] Using the ILO definition of unemployment.
Source: Labour Force Survey, Employment Department.

Young people's unemployment rates have risen and fallen alongside general unemployment since the 1970s but youth unemployment has been consistently higher (see Table 12), and the highs and lows have been considerably higher than in the 1950s and 60s. It used to be normal for school-leavers to have jobs arranged before their school-leaving dates. Likewise most university students decided which job offers to accept prior to graduation. Since the 1970s it has been normal for individuals to complete their full-time education with no known futures. When Howard Parker (1974) studied a group of young males in downtown Liverpool (a high unemployment district in a high unemployment city at that time, the early 1970s) unemployment was an option but rarely enforced. 'The boys' in Parker's study sometimes took 'holidays' immediately on school-leaving and 'breaks' between jobs, but obtaining another job was not difficult. At that time unemployment and job changing were highest among the same young people (Baxter 1975). The young unemployed were mostly individuals who were unwilling or unable to settle in the available jobs. Such career biographies are now rare. Labour market conditions no longer tolerate frequent job hopping.

Youth unemployment has been highest in the UK's high unemployment regions but, as Chapter One explained, regional differences have narrowed over time. Within all regions unemployment has been highest among the least qualified young people. They have suffered from restructuring—the decline of unskilled manufacturing jobs that less qualified school-leavers, especially males, formerly entered, and the conversion of girls' former full-time occupations into part-time jobs, most of which have gone to other social groups. The least qualified have also suffered from being at the back of 'the queue'. As competition for jobs has intensified, and as school-leavers' qualifications have improved, qualified job seekers have traded down the labour market to the special detriment of those on the lowest rungs with nowhere to descend to.

Up to the early 1980s surveys which recorded unemployment at above 50 per cent, or even around 30 percent within selected groups or neighbourhoods, commanded newspaper headlines. The normalization of these unemployment rates can be seen in that they are no longer news.

A breakdown of transitions?

The spread of youth unemployment in the 1970s was accompanied by cries of alarm. Unemployment was known to be damaging whatever the victims' ages but young people were considered especially vulnerable. Government measures to reduce unemployment were heavily targeted towards the young. It was said to be demoralizing for young people to leave school then find themselves unwanted. Such treatment was considered likely to lead to the young rejecting their society. There were forecasts of politically alienated youth being susceptible to appeals from the extreme left and right, and that those prevented from working when young would become unwilling or unable to work in the future. Allowing young people to adjust to lives without work was considered dangerous. Rising crime rates were forecast if large numbers of young people had time on their hands but no wages to spend. The social fabric was said to be at risk. Families and local communities as well as the wider economic and political systems were expected to wilt if high levels of unemployment, especially youth unemployment, persisted. Were these forecasts realistic or have they been disproved by subsequent experience?

An ordeal

All the relevant studies show that the vast majority of young people dislike being unemployed. 'Dislike' is really too weak a term to convey their feelings. In Leo Hendry and his colleagues' (1984) study of Scottish school-leavers an expression that many used to describe their experience of unemployment was 'an ordeal'. Some treated short spells of joblessness as vacations. Some maintained their hopes and spirits by making job hunting into a vocation. However, prolonged spells of unemployment were typically experienced as soul destroying. The young people complained of the boredom, the uncertainty of not knowing when the predicament would end, the demoralization of job applications that were rejected and sometimes never even acknowledged, being persistently short of money, and being denied normal leisure.

All inquiries that have incorporated widely used measurements of well-being such as the General Health Questionnaire have confirmed that youth (and adult) unemployment is damaging (Banks and Ullah 1988; Donovan and Oddy 1982; Jackson and Stafford 1980). Irrespective of whether people like their jobs, paid work is usually good for their mental health (Haworth 1993). Employment keeps people active, generates social contact, structures time, and gives people an acceptable status. The everyday acquainted question, 'What do you do?' is ordinarily taken to mean, 'What work?' An enquiry addressed to the unemployed in most casual social encounters is whether they have found work yet. Having to admit failure repeatedly is painful. It is work, not leisure activities, that is most likely to supply 'optimal experience'—the highs that are experienced when challenges are met successfully (Csikszentmihalyi 1990). Training schemes alleviate much of the psychological damage that unemployment otherwise inflicts, which is one reason why many young people rate even 'warehousing' schemes as better than nothing.

The significance of duration

Claire Wallace (1987) interviewed 153 school-leavers from Kent's Isle of Sheppey in 1979, followed up 103 after twelve months, and retained contact with some up to age 21. Nearly all the young people in this study had experienced unemployment. However, there were different experiences depending on the duration. Short spells did not appear to be damaging. In fact some young people complained just as vehemently about the quality of their jobs. In contrast, prolonged unemployment was never considered acceptable.

Other studies have confirmed that young people are able to tolerate and survive short spells out of work. Gaps between leaving school and first jobs may be treated as holidays. Periods of unemployment while changing jobs can be experienced as breaks. The individuals concerned usually regard themselves as 'between jobs' or 'looking for work' rather than 'unemployed'. Some regard intermittent employment, careers composed of jobs punctuated by breaks, as preferable to continuous employment in low-paid monotonous jobs (Roberts *et al.* 1982). However, these attitudes are most common in areas where it is easiest for individuals to return to work when they choose, as was the case in Liverpool in the early 1970s.

Since then young people's unemployment rate has been consistently higher than adults' but the typical duration of young people's unemployed spells has been shorter (see Table 13). The introduction of training schemes and new courses in education has helped to fragment youth unemployment. Because of this tendency for youth unemployment to be spread around in sub-employed (less than fully employed but not continuously unemployed) early careers, overall levels can reach 30 per cent among specific groups before long term unemployment begins to rise steeply (Roberts *et al.* 1981). The ability of young people to tolerate short spells, and the fact that the normal experience of youth unemployment has been of short duration, helps to explain why the alarmist forecasts of the 1970s and early 1980s have not materialised.

Table 13 Unemployed claimants: by duration, sex, and age, 1991[1] (United Kingdom)

Percentages and thousands

	Duration of unemployment (percentages)						Total (= 100%) (thousands)
	Up to 13 weeks	Over 13 up to 26 weeks	Over 26 up to 52 weeks	Over 52 up to 104 weeks	Over 104 up to 156 weeks	Over 156 weeks	
Males aged:							
18–19	48.2	24.3	20.7	6.8			119.6
20–4	38.4	22.1	20.9	11.9	3.8	2.8	345.4
25–34	34.4	20.1	19.6	13.5	4.8	7.6	502.8
35–49	32.6	18.7	17.5	12.9	4.7	13.5	417.9
50–9	25.4	14.8	14.5	11.6	5.8	28.0	240.7
60 and over	38.8	23.0	23.5	8.5	1.4	4.9	40.2
All males aged 18 and over	34.6	19.8	18.8	12.2	4.3	10.4	1,666.6
Females aged:							
18–19	51.3	23.1	19.9	5.6			65.8
20–4	45.2	21.6	19.1	9.0	2.6	2.6	128.3
25–34	43.2	20.8	20.5	8.9	2.5	4.2	136.4
35–49	40.7	18.4	17.8	11.6	3.9	7.6	120.0
50–9	25.1	13.3	15.1	12.4	6.5	27.6	77.8
60 and over	5.6	4.7	4.6	6.1	8.1	71.0	0.6
All females aged 18 and over	41.4	19.6	18.6	9.6	3.1	7.6	528.8

[1] At April.

Source: Employment Department.

Work values preserved

Young people usually survive unemployment with their work values, aspirations, and self-concepts intact. Experiencing joblessness does not usually cause them to revise their life plans. In 1984 Paul Willis followed *Learning to Labour* with a survey of 253 16–22-year-olds in Wolverhampton (Willis *et al.* 1988). At the time of this study a third of the age group in Wolverhampton was unemployed and this was reflected in the experiences of the young people in the survey. They were certainly not enjoying life on the dole. Rather, they resented their enforced dependence on their families and the state. They felt that their predicament was not only unpleasant but fundamentally wrong and immoral. They were angry rather than demoralized or apathetic. They had not abandoned their desire to work. In fact many of the males had very similar aspirations to 'the lads' in Willis's earlier study.

All the relevant studies have found that the young unemployed's work commitment, the importance attached to having a job, remains high. The ESRC 16–19 Initiative found that the desire for employment was actually strongest among the group at the greatest risk of unemployment, namely, the least qualified (Banks *et al.* 1992). Most unemployed young people are not just willing but eager to work. When asked about the types of jobs that they will accept a common answer is 'anything', which does not necessarily mean that those concerned have abandoned hope of obtaining decent jobs; they are simply willing to lower their sights temporarily in order to escape unemployment. The young unemployed's pay demands are typically modest. Many say that they will work for any sum above their benefit entitlement. White and McRae's (1989) survey of the long-term young unemployed found that the majority were flexible rather than rigid about the kinds of work that they would accept, and that their 'reservation wages', the minimum pay that they would accept, were so far beneath normal earnings that pay requirements could not have been a significant barrier to their employment. The England and Wales Youth Cohort Surveys have monitored the young unemployed's wage expectations regularly. Throughout the 1980s this evidence mirrored White and McRae's findings. However, the 1991 survey of 18–19-year-olds found, for the first time in the series, that the unemployed's average reservation wage exceeded the age group's average pay (Park 1994), but this has been an exceptional finding and no study has disputed the young unemployed's desire to work. The longitudinal evidence from the Scottish Young People's Surveys has shown that prolonged unemployment erodes young people's confidence in job searching but not their desire for employment (Furlong 1992).

It is not just the desire to work that survives unemployment but also, in most cases, young people's basic 'cognitive maps' of the world of work which indicate what one needs to do to reach a given destination. The 'ordinary kids' in Phil Brown's (1987) South Wales comprehensive schools completed their education believing that in order to obtain a decent job one needed to work hard and gain qualifications. What happened when such individuals did their best, passed examinations then found themselves or friends unemployed? Brown found that the young people usually held on to their convictions. Other people's unemployment was generally attributed to them never bothering to study or train. The young people attributed their own unemployment, when they found themselves in the predicament, either to a straightforward lack of jobs or their own lack of enough or the right qualifications.

Coping

F. COFFIELD, C. BORRILL, AND S. MARSHALL, *GROWING UP AT THE MARGINS* (Open University Press, Milton Keynes, 1986).

This book is based on qualitative fieldwork conducted between 1982 and 1984 which focused on fifty 16–25-year-olds, all of whom had substantial experience of unemployment. The young people were from three towns in North-East England which had all been severely affected by the decline of local industries. Unemployment had affected most families in the towns.

The young people featured in this study were pragmatists—they were eager for jobs, almost any jobs, even on modest wages.

Unemployment was experienced as a problem, a serious problem, but the young people had 'survival strategies' that enabled them to cope. Traditional community structures and cultures had survived in the towns where the young people lived. All generations were strongly attached to their region. Extended families were the norm. These were among the resources which were enabling the young people to endure unemployment without acute anguish and torment.

The extent to which families cushion the impact of youth unemployment has also been stressed by Susan Hutson and Richard Jenkins (1989) in their Swansea and Port Talbot study of fifty-eight families which contained a total of sixty-four unemployed 18–25-year-olds. Parents usually softened the financial impact of their children's unemployment while ensuring that the latter were treated like and felt like adults. Unemployment was a source of rows in some of the families. It caused financial and social strains. Parents often became annoyed at their children's inability to find work. Many of the households could ill afford grown-up dependants. Nevertheless, the young people were usually indulged, even spoilt, and family relationships remained close. The young people's families were usually 'taking the strain'. The result was that the young people were continuing to make near normal transitions to adulthood despite the interruptions of unemployment. Parents would encourage their children to keep looking for work, which could be a source of arguments, but it helped to prevent the young people regarding their unemployment as permanent. Parents could not fully compensate for their children's wagelessness but they usually ensured that the young people were not denied all normal leisure. Board would usually be charged, signifying the payer's adult status, then often given back during the week.

However, the effects of unemployment upon households can be complicated. The impact is likely to depend on the initial state of family relationships. The well-publicized problem of homelessness among young people in Britain is evidence that families do not always take the strain. And some young people have no families to depend on. The dissolution of marriages and the reconstitution of households can leave children, maybe especially teenagers, wondering where they belong and unable to feel that the places where they live are their real homes. Even otherwise 'normal' families can be vulnerable when exposed to stresses such as those associated with unemployment.

This is illustrated in Pat Allatt and Sue Yeandle's (1991) study of forty young adults and their families in Newcastle-upon-Tyne in the early 1980s. The parents in this study, as in the South Wales inquiry, were anxious to help their children, especially when the latter were experiencing unemployment. However, Allatt and Yeandle draw attention to the ways in which unemployment was undermining family relationships. Parents who were unemployed had no useful contacts through which to assist their children's job searching. The advice that parents gave often failed to work even when the children paid heed. Lives were being disorganized. The moral universe within which the families had lived was disintegrating. Parents were aware that they were being forced by circumstances to let standards slip by tacitly condoning idleness, dole fiddling, and even law breaking. Many of the parents feared that their unemployed children would be tempted or driven into crime, and felt unable to intervene effectively.

Allatt and Yeandle's evidence poses questions about whether young people's ability to cope and survive unemployment without long-term damage to their personalities or careers might decline over time. Most of the young people who experienced unemployment in the 1970s and 80s were not scarred for life. Studies of the subsequent lives of individuals who were affected by unemployment before the Second World War, when they left school, have testified to young people's powers of recovery (Cameron *et al.* 1943; Elder 1974; Travers 1986). When they obtain jobs young people's mental health usually returns to normal levels. Rather than being especially vulnerable, young people are probably better able to cope with unemployment than older age groups. The young unemployed can realistically expect to obtain work in a not too distant future. Even those who experience repeated unemployment can also experience a gradual improvement in their positions—in the types of jobs that they are able to obtain, the remuneration, and their treatment by their families. Young people can normally rely on family support during spells of unemployment. Victims of economic restructuring in their forties and fifties, people with family responsibilities but with little hope of regaining their former occupational status, have more reason to feel that their entire lives have been shattered. But what will happen in the longer term if persistent unemployment undermines the support systems which, up to now, have enabled most young people to cope? Allatt and Yeandle (1991) have drawn attention to these destructive tendencies. During the 1970s and 80s most young people may have coped with their typically short spells of unemployment but for some there were no happy endings. Some left their schools and schemes and then became long-term unemployed save for periods on further special measures. In high unemployment regions and cities such as Liverpool a fifth or more of all young people have been growing into their twenties without establishing themselves in any regular employment (Roberts *et al.* 1987). Will families cope if this situation is repeated through several generations by which time many of the young unemployed's parents will themselves be long-term unemployed?

An emerging British underclass?

Raising this question leads into the debate on whether Britain has an underclass, a section of the population situated beneath the lower ranks of the employed work-force. Verdicts on this question inevitably depend on how an underclass is defined.

In the late 1980s Michelle Connolly and her colleagues at Liverpool University surveyed a representative sample of black youth in Liverpool

Table 14 Liverpool: positions thirty months beyond fifth form (in percentages)

	Main sample (1988)	Ethnic minority (1989)
Education	22	18
Schemes	1	3
Full-time job	45	21
Part-time job	7	2
Unemployed	22	52
Other	4	5

Source: Connolly *et al.* (1991).

(Connolly *et al.* 1991). This sample was selected, and the interview schedule was designed, so that the findings would be comparable with evidence from the ESRC 16–19 Initiative which was simultaneously investigating a representative sample of all-Liverpool youth. The unemployment rate among Liverpool's young blacks was twice as high as among all the city's young people, and youth unemployment in Liverpool was higher than in any of the other areas studied in the ESRC 16–19 Initiative (Kirkcaldy, Sheffield, and Swindon). This meant that young blacks in Liverpool were twice as likely to be unemployed as to have full-time jobs (see Table 14). At age 18–19, 52 per cent of Liverpool's young blacks were unemployed while only 21 per cent had full-time jobs. This study proceeded to discuss whether Liverpool's young blacks, or a proportion of them, could be considered an underclass and argued that for this term to be applied four conditions should be met.

(i) The group should be disadvantaged relative to, and in this sense beneath, the lowest stratum of the employed working population.

(ii) For the individuals and families involved this situation should be persistent.

(iii) The underclass should be separate from other groups in social and cultural respects as well as in its lack of regular employment. For example, its members might belong to separate social networks, live in separate areas, and have their own distinctive lifestyles.

(iv) The culture of the underclass, whether developed to cope, adjust, or resist, should be another impediment, and sufficient in itself to significantly reduce its members' likelihood of joining the regularly employed work-force even if other obstacles were removed.

Young people are a critical group for deciding whether an underclass has formed or is emerging in Britain. From their experiences, attitudes, and ways of life it should be possible to establish whether subcultures that separate such a group from the employed population are being transmitted down the generations.

Up to now most British sociologists who have considered the underclass theory have rejected the concept. However, some of these rejections have been based on improbable constructions of the form that an underclass would take. There is no evidence of Britain acquiring a politically radical underclass, but this does not rule out there being an underclass with different characteristics. The groups situated beneath the employed population are socially and culturally diverse. They are divided by sex, age, lifestyles, ethnicity, and other circumstances. Some groups are antagonistic towards others but this has applied to sections of the working class. We can rule out there being a solidaristic underclass, but should solidarity be among the definitive features?

Some sociologists' resistance to the underclass theory appears at least partly ideological. Sociologists have vested professional interests in their orthodox class schemes. Some may have been reluctant to acknowledge that the working class could have a potential enemy beneath, and that the least advantaged might have interests that differ from those of the working class. Many sociologists have been critical of the ways in which underclass theories, like earlier culture of poverty and cycle of deprivation theories, appear to blame the victims. Such explanations may appeal to and be ideologically convenient for the advantaged, who are thereby relieved of blame. However, the ideological and political implications of underclass theories are not strictly relevant to their factual validity.

Many sociologists have been hostile to what is probably the best-known version of the underclass theory, that of Charles Murray (1990), an American social scientist, who has charted in detail the creation of an underclass in the USA and claims to detect similar developments in Britain. Murray identifies welfare dependence as a primary cause, rather than a consequence, of the existence of an underclass and his favoured solution, therefore, involves tougher welfare regimes. Murray also claims that single mothers are deeply implicated in the perpetuation of the underclass and advocates welfare regimes which will enable or force all sections of the population to recognize the benefits of conventional family life. Many British sociologists have been critical of conventional families and would prefer to enable single parents to cope more effectively rather than pressure them into dependence on male partners. Once again, however, ideological objections to a point of view do not amount to factual refutation.

It is safe to conclude that most young people who experience unemployment do not thereby become members of an underclass. In most cases unemployment prolongs and complicates but does not undermine normal economic and other types of socialization. It is also the case that no large-scale survey of young people in Britain has identified an underclass. However, this could be due to the under-class being too small and heterogeneous to have sufficient represen-tatives to stand out as a distinguishable stratum even in large samples, or because underclass members tend to be non-respon-dents. The highest response rates in surveys of young people are always from the best educated. And there are several strands of evidence of underclass formation in Britain that simply cannot be ignored.

The long-term unemployed

Some young people's unemployment is not just a short-term problem. Among certain groups long-term unemployment is common. The black young people in Liverpool studied by Michelle Connolly and her colleagues (1991) were one such group. This investigation concluded that the young blacks could not be described as an underclass because the vast majority retained conventional job aspirations. However, the book also argued that the patience of Liverpool's black population might not be indefinite. Much the same might be said of the coping strategies and resilience of other chronically unemployed groups, espe-cially when their resilience has drawn upon the support of family and neighbourhood structures and cultures that developed when most adults (the males at any rate) had jobs.

Disappearing from the system

Some young people lose contact with mainstream social institutions and become invisible to official data collection and orthodox social sur-veys. Homeless young people who squat or live in 'cardboard cities' are well-known examples. It is impossible to say precisely how many there are, or what happens to them eventually. Some young people attend spasmodically, if at all, during the final years of compulsory education. Some become statistically invisible when they leave full-time education officially at age 16, do not obtain jobs or enter training schemes, and have no incentive to register because they are ineligible for social security.

A detailed analysis of all the available evidence from South Glamorgan in 1993 indicated that at any point in time between 16 and 22 per cent of all 16- and 17-year-olds in the region were not in education, training, or employment (Istance *et al.* 1994). Some were only temporarily 'missing', but a hardcore was permanently 'lost'. Members of this hardcore tended to be from broken homes and from a limited number of schools where they had usually been chronic non-attenders, and they were in fact known to the social services, police, and courts. Interviews with twenty-six such young people suggested that if they were not already into crime they had turned to it as a necessary source of income since officially leaving full-time education.

The unemployable

This term is used widely by Careers Service and Jobcentre staff even though it is never used in government reports. The term is unscientific and ideologically loaded but probably socially realistic in suggesting that some unemployed individuals are unlikely to be recruited by any employer. The reasons why individuals are considered unemployable may be due to their limited physical or mental abilities, personality traits, or lifestyles which involve persistent drug use, for example.

Despite the rise in educational attainments around 8 per cent of young people still leave school completely unqualified. Around 12 per cent of 21-year-olds report difficulties with their spelling, writing, reading, or number work and this percentage has not declined in recent years (Ekinsmyth and Bynner 1994). Such young people are among those most at risk of unemployment.

Whether or not a particular type of person is employable or unemployable may depend on the balance between labour market demand and supply. In times of full employment lack of qualifications, a criminal history, or a record of chronic job instability may not be barriers to further employment. When employers can pick and choose, as has been the case in most parts of the UK when hiring unskilled labour since the mid-1970s, would-be workers at the back of the queue may be unemployable for all practical purposes. Another argument is that jobs have become more demanding due to a combination of technical change and competitive pressures which have forced employers to insist on higher standards, thereby raising the threshold beneath which individuals are unemployable.

Hustling for a living

Crime is some young people's normal source of income. 'Soft' drugs are widely available and used. Recreational drug use does not place anyone in an underclass but some addicted 'hard' drug users need to steal regularly to finance their habit. Others make livelihoods from the trade.

It is difficult to identify these subcultures in questionnaire surveys. Informal observation and participation can be more successful in these respects. Throughout the 1980s Steve Craine (1994) maintained contact with thirty-nine young people who left school completely unqualified in a particular Manchester district. A small minority of the subjects made 'traditional transitions' into employment on leaving school. They were mostly from 'respectable' families in their working-class neighbourhood, used informal contacts to obtain their jobs, and aimed to 'get out' of the district and 'get on' in the wider society. Another minority had made 'protracted transitions' via schemes and periods of unemployment. Most came from families with role models of work commitment and the young people had a 'getting in' frame of reference. However, the largest group had left school and subsequently became long-term or repeatedly unemployed. These young people tended to be from their district's roughest estate and the majority had unemployed parents. By their mid-twenties most of this group had effectively withdrawn from the labour market. The females had withdrawn into domestic roles, though not as part of conventional families. The males' lifestyles needed freedom from domestic commitments. Their means of earning included working 'off the cards' and various forms of 'hustling', always involving some breach of the law or social security fiddle. Some made livings from shop-lifting, drug dealing, and armed theft. Most of these males had at least one conviction.

The young people studied by Steve Craine were not representative of all residents in their district, and their district was not a representative part of Manchester or anywhere else. It is impossible to say exactly how many young people nationwide are represented by the subjects in Craine's research. The crucial point for present purposes is that such young people exist, they are not purely fictional characters, and unemployment is part of the context in which they develop and sustain their ways of life.

Unconventional families

All the relevant studies show that young people with unemployed parents are less successful at school and have higher rates of subsequent unemployment than those whose parents are in work. Children who are reared by single parents are also less successful at school and subsequently in the labour market than those reared by two parents (Roberts *et al.* 1987). This is not to say that all unemployed or single parents are bad parents. Nor is it to deny that in many instances single parent situations are more satisfactory for the children and adults than the preceding situations of domestic conflict. Nevertheless, the overall statistical relationships are beyond dispute. The processes whereby children of unemployed and single parents become disadvantaged are controversial but the crucial point for present purposes is that, whatever the processes, the relationships exist. It is also the case that unemployed teenagers are more likely to become teenage parents, typically single parents, than either full-time students or contemporaries who are in employment (Payne 1987; Penhale 1989). Again, the reasons for these relationships are open to debate. They are likely to include the shortage of male breadwinners in the social networks of the young women who become single parents. Whatever the responsible processes, the point is that people with disadvantaged family origins tend to repeat the cycle with their own children and unemployment is among the relevant contextual features.

The case for the existence of an underclass in Britain may still be not proven but there are many indications that such a stratum could be in the making. Its creation is more likely to be a long-term consequence of persistent unemployment than an immediate effect. In the early twentieth century social researchers used terms such as 'loafers', 'the idle', and 'the criminal classes' when categorizing young people's social backgrounds. Social science today is more sophisticated but another reason why the use of these terms lapsed is that society changed. Throughout the twentieth century up to the 1960s the 'lower orders' in Britain were being incorporated into mainstream society through the provision of welfare services and, after the Second World War, by the availability of jobs and rising wage levels, especially for the unskilled. Since the 1960s the former trends have been reversed. Britain has become more polarized. Over several generations a consequence is likely to be the recreation of 'lower orders'. A fully formed underclass may still be just a future possibility but by the early 1990s various strands of evidence were at least consistent with such a-class being in the making.

Aspirations, self-concepts, and opportunities

Unemployment has certainly complicated, but probably without undermining or even changing the basic processes of occupational socialization for the majority of young people. Only a small minority are even at risk of becoming part of an underclass. A more widespread, but less obvious change has been the raising of young people's ambitions above their actual employment opportunities.

This has happened partly through *stratified diffusion*, the downward spread of ideas once present only in the higher socio-economic strata. Working-class families, certainly a substantial proportion of them, have absorbed the success ideology. These parents now tell their children that they should study for qualifications in order to 'get on'. Since the spread of comprehensive schools these messages have spread beyond the minority who passed the 11-plus. Parents and teachers now preach the success ideology to boys and girls from all social backgrounds. This was evident in the ethnographies in the ESRC 16-19 Initiative (see Bates and Riseborough 1993). The boys who were training to work in the building trades, and the girls who were training for care occupations, were nearly all from working-class homes, but so were many of the students on the BTEC courses which, they hoped, would lead to careers in fashion design and hotel management.

A parallel development helping to lift young people's career sights has been their rising stay-on rates and increasing success in gaining educational qualifications. Young people are encouraged to study for qualifications so as to obtain good jobs. And when they have earned the qualifications they usually expect jobs as good as those entered by earlier school- and college-leavers with similar attainments. Paradoxically, the later cohorts' own behaviour makes this impossible; too many try to emulate the success stories from earlier cohorts and there is insufficient room at or near the top to accommodate them all.

Notwithstanding all the qualifications mentioned previously, all the studies conducted among Britain's school-leavers up to the 1970s broadly endorsed Ashton and Field's conclusion that young people's family and educational backgrounds usually aligned their ambitions with the levels of employment that they were able to enter, and that once in employment young workers were exposed to occupational socialization which usually crystallized their aims on the particular kinds of jobs that they had obtained. Britain's school-leavers were mostly realistic and accommodating. In contrast, subsequent inquiries have found most beginning workers failing to obtain not just the particular jobs, but the levels of employment that they were hoping for. This applies from less qualified 16-year-olds who have found their options limited to schemes and 'trash jobs' rather than secure occupations paying adult wages, to university graduates who have been unable to embark on graduate careers, that is, careers for which a university degree is an essential requirement (Roberts *et al.* 1987). There has been no shortage of young people wanting to be trained up. Rather, young workers' most common complaint is that they receive insufficient training and are denied career prospects (Roberts and Chadwick 1991). The only training that young people *en bloc* reject is on schemes which lead nowhere.

School-leavers with unrealistic aspirations are not an entirely new phenomenon. There were always some individuals whose hopes were dashed when they entered the labour market. Since the 1960s investigations among black youth have consistently found that, compared with the white population, their vocational aspirations have been higher while their educational attainments have been lower (see, for example, Beetham 1967; Connolly *et al.* 1991). The black–white aspiration gap has been especially wide among young females (Driver 1980; Fuller 1980; Mirza 1992; Sargant 1993). The most likely explanations have been that the blacks' parents, especially the first generation immigrants who typically experienced occupational demotion on entering Britain, have been more ambitious for their children than white parents of equal occupational status (in Britain), and the black community's exaggerated confidence in even modest educational qualifications opening career opportunities (Roberts *et al.* 1981). Since the 1970s disenchantment with the opportunities encountered on entering the labour market seems to have spread throughout the white population.

Trying harder

There are several possible types of response when school-leavers' ambitions are thwarted. One is to persist with the 'getting on' strategy and to try even harder, which usually means staying even longer in education and gaining even better qualifications. This tactic can work for individuals provided only a few try it. When adopted by too many it only defers and ultimately aggravates the mismatch problem.

Cooling-out

Another possibility is that young workers' aspirations are 'cooled-out', that is, scaled down into line with their real opportunities. These processes were evident among the Sheffield YTS girls studied by Inge Bates (1993*a*) who were training to become care workers. The majority had initially wanted to work with children whereas they soon discovered that most of the care jobs available to young women such as themselves were with older people. This work was anything but glamorous. At first many of the trainees found the work revolting. They had to cope with sometimes violent, sometimes incontinent old people, and to confront death. However, while in training the majority developed a pride in their ability to cope, in not being 'bleeding whining Minnies'. Simultaneously, they reinvented their ambitions in line with their actual labour market opportunities and rethought their biographies in terms of choice.

Goal displacement

Another possibility is for individuals with blocked ambitions to displace their personal goals onto their children as they move into adulthood. Such displacement was common among first generation black immigrant parents in Britain. However, for most beginning workers this opportunity remains years away.

Role distancing

A further strategy is for young people to distance their self-concepts from their actual jobs and training. This type of role distancing is certainly not unprecedented, but in recent years it appears to have become a common mode of occupational adjustment among many groups of young people. Instead of celebrating their transitions into unskilled jobs like the lads studied by Paul Willis in the 1970s, in recent years many young workers have been distancing their real selves from the 'trash jobs' and 'slave labour' that they have been obliged to accept on account of needing the money and lacking alternatives (Roberts *et al.* 1982). This type of role distancing is not confined to unskilled workers. The BTEC fashion design students, another of Inge Bates's (1993*b*) case study groups in Sheffield, had aspirations towards jet-setting careers as designers with flats in London, Paris, and Rome. The more prosaic reality was that most would be employed as pattern cutters, machinists, and suchlike if they entered the fashion industry. Others would find work in garages, shops, and offices. The students were aware of their real prospects, but many were determined to cling to the aim, and to their conceptions of themselves, as potential international designers.

There was a similar separation between the immediate labour market realities facing the Sheffield BTEC group on the hotels and catering course that George Riseborough (1993*a*) studied and the students' aims. Most were intent on careers in hotel management or self-employment, though some wanted to become chefs. Many of the students were dismissive towards the lower level skills that their course demanded that they acquire. The attendance rate was just 60 per cent. This group were not highly committed students. Their course was basically a means to an end. So were the part-time, though in practice sometimes virtually full-time paid jobs in which the students were employed simultaneously in hotel and restaurant kitchens and dining rooms. In these jobs, as when at college, the young people were prepared to conform outwardly while preserving quite different conceptions of the employment for which they were really suited and which they hoped to enter eventually. If they failed to do this, as was likely for many in the group, they would be able to spend their working lives in jobs where they simply 'played the parts' while retaining different conceptions of themselves.

Occupational socialization may have changed least among young people on working-class trajectories, provided they have been able to obtain reasonably stable employment. The care girls whom Inge Bates (1993*a*) studied were mostly adjusting their aims to their real job prospects. The boys that George Riseborough (1993*b*) studied on a course which, they hoped, would lead to careers in the building trades, bore a close resemblance to the lads in Paul Willis's earlier research. The working-class jobs open to school-leavers have declined in number, but when working-class early school-leavers 'get in' their inclination seems to be to celebrate their good fortune and hang on, economically and psychologically. Occupational socialization has probably changed most for young people who want to 'get on'. Learning to distance oneself from one's work role seems to have become a common, perhaps the normal, mode of occupational socialization among this group. Whether this new normality is one aspect of a broader post-modern or late-modern social condition is considered in the next chapter.

Further reading

P. Willis (1977), *Learning to Labour*, Saxon House, Farnborough, is a classic study with arguments that remain relevant, if still controversial, two decades after the research was completed. For more recent accounts of young people coming to terms with the new labour market conditions of the 1980s and 1990s see I. Bates and G. Riseborough (eds.), (1993), *Youth and Inequality*, Open University Press, Buckingham; F. Coffield, C. Borrill and S. Marshall (1986), *Growing Up at the Margins*, Open University Press, Milton Keynes; and S. Hutson and R. Jenkins (1989), *Taking the Strain*, Open University Press, Milton Keynes.

Chapter Five

Individualization and Risk

Choice or opportunity?

In the 1960s and 70s there was much debate among sociologists and psychologists about whether the entry into employment was governed primarily by choice or opportunity. Choice theorists recognized that people could choose only from the jobs in their localities that were open to individuals with their particular qualifications. They also recognized that choices themselves were influenced by social factors such as family backgrounds and education. Nevertheless, they argued that most young people had some scope for choice, and that individuals based their choices partly on their own abilities and interests (see Daws 1977). It was also argued that, on the basis of their own preferences, individuals could sometimes change the boundaries of the occupations to which they had access, by migrating or becoming better qualified for instance. While individuals' choices were influenced by their social backgrounds and immediate circumstances it was argued that young people had some scope to select the circumstances which then became socializing influences. Work entry problems were attributed to young people failing to make the best possible choices and the remedy prescribed was better job information and advice. Vocational guidance was considered the key to enabling individuals to develop choices which achieved the closest possible fit between their own interests and abilities on the one hand, and labour market possibilities on the other. And what was good for individuals was said to be good for the entire economy.

Opportunity theorists, including the present writer (Roberts 1968, 1975, 1977) stressed that many school-leavers' scope for choice was extremely limited. Those with the widest scope, the best qualified, were faced by occupations that were so clearly stratified in terms of desirability as to make the best choices self-evident. It was argued that the best way to predict the types of employment that school-leavers would enter was in terms of the opportunities to which they had access as by virtue of their family backgrounds, sex, places of residence, and educational attainments. Many young people's scope for choice was dismissed as trivial. Attention was drawn to how most young people's ambitions settled on particular occupations only after these had been entered, and how, prior to entering the work-force, individuals' aims and self-concepts were already socially patterned and thereby, in most cases, aligned with the levels of employment to which they would have access. So-called choices were said to be mainly products of individuals' opportunities rather than vice versa. Opportunity theorists implied that vocational information, advice and guidance could make little difference to individuals' eventual destinations. At best they lubricated the transition, and smoothed and speeded young people's progress to their pre-ordained futures.

During the last twenty years this choices versus opportunity debate has subsided. The arguments were not won decisively by either side. Rather, the terms of the old debate have been criticized, and in some ways the arguments have become outdated. First, it has been argued on empirical grounds, on the basis of evidence, that the importance of choice (or action or agency) on the one hand, and the structure of opportunity on the other, has always varied between different groups of young people. Layder and his colleagues (1991) have shown that in recent years individuals' own characteristics have worked best when predicting entry to top jobs and have been least successful in predicting entry to training schemes. Structural factors, such as the unemployment rates in given localities, have been the best predictors of which school-leavers will enter Youth Training.

Secondly, it has been argued theoretically that both agency (choice) and structure are always implicated in social processes. Evetts (1992) has argued that careers acquire and retain their structured, 'given' characters only while people believe that the structures exist and act so as to reproduce them. Even when the jobs that young people enter are far from what they hoped for, their choices can still be important in explaining how they accept, adjust, and settle, or eventually quit their occupations. This was illustrated in Inge Bates's (1993a) study of young women on the Sheffield training scheme that fed into care occupations, mostly in residential accommodation for older people. This was not the kind of work that the young women had wanted at their time of school-leaving, but while on the training scheme the majority came to believe that the work was right for them. These 'choices' could not be ignored in explaining why the young women stayed on the training scheme and, in most cases, progressed into care employment.

A third, and perhaps the most fundamental reason why the old choice versus opportunity debate has lapsed, is that the process of work entry has changed. No one has seriously tried to explain most youth unemployment as a choice, but the prolonging of transitions has enabled nearly all young people to make some significant career choices: whether to remain in education at age 16 and, if so, whether to seek more academic or vocational qualifications, or whether to enter Youth Training, or to search for a job. Needless to say, these choices have not usually settled the occupations which individuals have eventually entered.

The new terminology

Choice versus opportunity has now been replaced by a new set of debates in which the keywords include individualization, uncertainty, and risk. Merely introducing this terminology is controversial in British sociology. The implication is that recent changes have been sufficiently fundamental to require new keywords. This is the contention of writers who describe the current economy as post-Fordist, and the wider society, or the one that we are becoming, as post-modern, late modern or high modern. Previous chapters have stressed the continuities in transitions into employment up to and since the 1970s. The main routes to good jobs and who gets them may not be fundamentally different. Even so, there have been changes.

The new terminology was developed initially by German sociologists, most of whom have been optimistic about the changes in young people's situations. The basic causes of the changes in Germany have been similar to those operating in Britain—economic restructuring, higher unemployment, and pressure from young people and their parents who want the qualifications that lead to good jobs, for example. However, whereas the tendency in British sociology and political debate has been to see the trends as creating problems for young people, in Germany the trends have been greeted with optimism. British researchers have written about school-leavers' broken bridges and have drawn attention to the 'limbo' into which many have been thrust. In Germany longer transitions have been welcomed as creating a moratorium within which young people can take stock of themselves and their situations, then purposively shape their own futures. Another difference is that in Britain the changes have led to much questioning of the country's basic approaches in education and training. The outcomes of this questioning have included new courses in education and new training schemes. In Germany, in contrast, national confidence in the country's education and training arrangements—tripartite secondary education followed by higher education or apprentice training—has been virtually unscathed. German responses to any breakdowns in young people's transitions, therefore, have taken the form of tinkering, consolidating, and sometimes expanding the familiar rather than inventing new courses, qualifications, and schemes (Rose and Page 1989).

Individualization

Individualization is an example of a word that needed to be coined before people could become aware that it was happening all around them. Once its meaning is understood, the concept is immediately seen to be useful, or so its users (including the present author) believe. Indeed, observers sometimes begin seeing individualization everywhere. This trend is alleged to be affecting all age groups but with young people at the forefront.

A crude measure of individualization is the proportion of age peers in a person's social network with whom he or she shares a common biography having grown up in the same district, attended the same schools, and entered similar types of employment at the same ages. Virtually everything that every individual does and experiences is still shared with many other people, but nowadays in a variety of individualized sequences and combinations. Individualization reduces the numbers of persons whose biographies match closely those of most other members of any social category, whether defined by gender, type of school attended, or family background.

Individualization is not an entirely new development. Writers who use the concept argue that it is a very long-term process that began with the replacement of traditional by modern society. Industrial employment has always been of individuals. In modern democracies it has always been individuals, not families or any other groups, that have been able to vote. However, it can be argued that recently the longer-term process has accelerated and crossed a threshold which has required 'individualization' to be adopted as a key sociological concept.

Several trends are held responsible for individualizing young people's situations. First, longer transitions into employment and towards adulthood more generally have led to young people progressing through various forms of post-compulsory education and training, interspersed with periods in full-time and part-time jobs, and spells of unemployment, in a huge variety of sequences.

A second, even more important development has been the breakup of the concentrations of employment in the firms and industries that once dominated many local labour markets. In the 1960s Rawstron and Coates (1966) drew attention to the unusually narrow ranges of employment that were available for school-leavers in places such as Bradford, where 31 per cent of all jobs were in textiles, Stoke-on-Trent, where 34 per cent of all jobs were in ceramics, and Barrow, where ship-building and marine engineering accounted for 41 per cent of all employment. These concentrations of employment were once seen as restricting local youth's scope for choice. School-leavers' problems in all these places since the 1960s have arisen partly through the decline of the traditionally dominant industries. Most local labour markets today offer wider ranges of employment. There was never a time or place where absolutely every young male in the village went down the pit, or where every girl was employed in the local textile mill. However, in the past, in many parts of Britain, there were major types of employment which most school-leavers of a given age and sex could expect to enter. Some individuals always broke out. In the past, in many parts of the country, such young people were exceptional. Today what were once the normal patterns have gone, and virtually every young person has become exceptional.

Higher rates of residential mobility have been a third individualizing trend. A fourth has been the development of more diverse lifestyles within each gender but especially among women. There is no longer a clear normal pattern to women's lives. Formerly most women worked full-time until they married and became mothers when they withdrew from the labour market. The majority subsequently returned, usually to part-time jobs, often at lower levels than the occupations that they had previously held. Some women's lives still match this pattern but there are now more single parents, and on becoming mothers more women are taking maternity leave rather than terminating their employment. A fifth set of changes which will have accentuated individualization has been the increasing instability of marriages and families, and the weakening of neighbourhood and religious communities.

Individualization has reduced the scope for traditional youth ethnography. It used to be possible for researchers to establish contact with, and sometimes to become participant observers in (usually male) groups of teenagers in selected areas, and to identify typical features in their biographies, current situations, attitudes, and lifestyles. This methodology no longer yields the same returns. There are fewer neighbourhood peer groups because most neighbourhoods have lost the cohesion that was born of residential immobility and common experiences and opportunities. Needless to say, there are still some traditional pockets, but nowadays youth ethnographers are more likely to contact their subjects in colleges and training schemes, as Inge Bates and George Riseborough did in the ESRC 16–19 Initiative, or at discos (Evans 1989). However, these contact points tend to be places where the populations are constantly replenished and those present at any time are often from diverse backgrounds and head towards different destinations. Qualitative research among today's young people is more likely to based on case studies, as in Allatt and Yeandle's studies of unemployed teenagers in the North-East (see page 97), rather than real peer groups.

Active and passive individualization

In their comparative study of young people in Britain and Germany in the early 1990s Karen Evans and Walter Heinz (1994) distinguished active from passive individualization. The distinction was found in both countries, as was the association between active individualization and academic success.

Active individualization occurs when individuals form goals early on, to become a medical doctor for example, then take all the steps that are necessary to reach the goal. It is hardly surprising that the Anglo-German study found that this kind of individualization was most common on high status career routes. We have seen that these are the routes on which outcomes are most predictable from individuals' own characteristics (Layder *et al.* 1991). Academically successful young people from advantaged families have the best opportunities to become active individualizers. There seems to be a tendency for young people to project their own experiences on to the wider society. So, academically successful young people tend to give answers which place them towards the internal pole on 'locus of control' scales when questioned about whether economic events and outcomes are determined by individuals or their circumstances (Banks *et al.* 1992).

The young people who, in terms of the earlier debate, would have been portrayed with the least scope for choice, are nowadays said to be passively individualized. In the Anglo-German study they were not necessarily passive at any critical career junctures, but in so far as they took or rejected opportunities as these arose rather than implemented preformed plans their biographies tended to be constructed primarily by circumstances.

Both passive and active individualization are likely to make young people conscious of how they differ from, rather than the experiences and interests that they share with large numbers of others. This type of individualized consciousness is likely to be accompanied by feelings of personal responsibility for one's own current condition, whatever this might be, and for constructing one's own future. This consciousness is strongest and most prevalent among individuals on high status career routes, but the Anglo-German study found that it was the norm among young Britons and Germans on all the main career routes in each country (Roberts *et al.* 1994).

Destructuration or structured fragmentation?

Some writers, most notably the German optimists, have linked individualization to a destructuring of young people's situations. They have argued that prolonged transitions create a 'moratorium' during which young people can escape from the old determinants of their life chances such as gender, social class origins, and achievements in secondary education. Having recognized their autonomy young people are supposed to decide the types of adults they wish to become, control their own subsequent socialization by taking the right courses and acquiring the necessary qualifications and skills, then build their preferred futures (Zinneker 1990). In other words, from youth and young adulthood onwards active individualization is supposed to become the norm, and this is equated with young people escaping from former structural constraints.

In practice, however, we have seen that the evidence shows that opportunities for active individualization occur mainly among young people in relatively privileged situations. Chapter Three explained that the old predictors of employment outcomes remain in excellent working order in Britain, and the same seems to apply in Germany (Evans and Heinz 1994). Young people's situations and future prospects continue to be governed by their family origins, gender and places of residence.

An alternative view is that individualization is not a product of these divisions dissolving or losing their influence. Rather, individualization arises through structured fragmentation. The old determinants of life chances continue to operate but in a variety of individualized configurations. Multivariate analysis of survey data and qualitative deconstruction of individuals' career biographies can reveal the persistent links. However, young people themselves will be less likely than formerly to recognize the advantages and disadvantages that they share with most others of the same gender, from the same kind of schools, who live in the same localities, and so on. The result is that social divisions become opaque and aggregates such as social classes cease to feel that they share sufficient in common which distinguishes them from other groups to nurture solidaristic sentiments and conceptions of mutual interests.

Uncertain destinations

Individualization *per se* renders young people's later destinations obscure. When one knows the social group in which one belongs it is relatively easy to look ahead and see what one's future holds. The situations of older members of the group will normally give clear indications. However, additional trends have been blurring young people's futures. The sheer pace of economic, technological, and occupational change means that few careers can any longer be relied on to last until retirement. The increased instability of economic life is almost certainly connected, albeit in complex ways, to the fact that family life is also less stable than formerly and marriages can no longer be relied on to last for life.

It is not just the distant future that has become difficult to predict. Young people in education and training can no longer be certain of their next steps. Recently introduced courses, training schemes, and qualifications have no established track records, but it is not just the less qualified's futures that have become uncertain. The increased numbers on longer established routes, in higher education for example, means that they cannot all enter traditionally commensurate jobs. The best qualified can no longer be confident of 'glittering prizes'.

Risk

This means that all the career steps that individuals might take involve risk. The outcomes are no longer sufficiently predictable for individuals to feel secure. The 'risk' concept, like individualization, has been introduced into sociology by German writers, particularly Ulrich Beck (1992). He has drawn attention to how the possibility of ecological and nuclear disasters means that we all now live in a world of risks. However, these are not risks over which most individuals have any leverage.

The more pertinent sense in which young people today make their ways into risk societies is that they have to make decisions, to take steps, which will almost certainly affect their future opportunities, but where the outcomes are moderate probabilities at best. Unless a young German completes an apprenticeship it is most unlikely that he or she will ever become a skilled worker, but completing an apprenticeship will not make it equally likely that the person will obtain a skilled job. Even if such employment is obtained the occupation may not outlast the individual's working life. There is really no way in which anyone today can be certain. An employer-based training scheme in Britain may lead to a good job offer or back to unemployment. A university degree may lead to high rising management or professional career, but an entrant to higher education today would be unwise to bank on such a future. In a similar way, marriage may lead to lifetime domestic and emotional security but it may also lead to personal despair. There is simply no way in which today's young people can avoid risk taking.

Needless to say, the future has never been 100 per cent predictable. The key changes are that uncertainty has increased, and in individual-ized societies it is individuals who have to take the crucial risks with their own lives. They take the decisions and reap the rewards or pay the penalties. It is as if people nowadays embarked on their life journeys without reliable maps, all in private motor cars rather than the trains and buses in which entire classes once travelled together. These analo-gies are another product of recent German sociology (see Berger *et al.* 1993). The 'cars' in which individuals now travel do not all have equally powerful engines. Some young people have already accumulated advantages in terms of economic assets and socio-cultural capital. Some have to travel by bicycle or on foot. But everyone has to take risks. No one can be certain where the roads that they can take will lead. For those on the bicycles the risks may be between non-skilled jobs and unemployment. Those entering higher education may run far lower risks of future joblessness but the social distance is typically much wider between the heights that they might realistically attain and the more modest futures that await many.

From life cycle to life course

The old certainties that have been lost include those of major life events occurring in a definite and predictable order during prescribed life stages. Childhood and youth used to be for education and training, and selecting marital partners. These used to be the life stages when indi-viduals prepared for adulthood. As adults they normally established themselves in occupational careers and families. Then came the life stages of disengagement. Lives today are less tidy. Adults whose work-ing lives have been disrupted may return to education or training. Chapter One explained that much of Britain's recent increase in student numbers in higher education has been due to the growth in mature entrants. This can be seen in Table 15. During the 1980s there was only a small increase, just 8 per cent, in the number of young students in Britain's older universities, whereas mature students grew by 40 per cent. In the polytechnics and colleges which subsequently became Britain's new universities there was more rapid all-round growth but, once again, especially in the mature age groups. The loosening of the links between education and age is just one way in which the traditional life cycle has been dislocated. Marital instability means that falling in love is no longer just for the young. Some individuals succumb repeatedly and it has become common to encounter 40- and 50-year-olds emulating 'swinging' adolescent lifestyles. Hence the talk of the destandardization of the life cycle.

Table 15 Great Britain: first degree full-time home first year students (in 000s)

	1980	1985	1990	% age change 1980–90
Universities				
Young	69.0	62.9	74.2	8
Mature	7.6	6.8	10.6	40
	76.6	69.7	84.8	
Polytechnics and colleges				
Young	34.9	46.4	67.2	93
Mature	9.6	11.8	24.1	152
	44.5	58.2	91.3	

However, there is still a life course and it is probably as misleading to talk of complete destandardization as a destructuring of young people's situations. 'Anything goes' in any life stage has not become the new rule. It has not become possible to tackle major life events in any order. Age remains a powerful basis for social discrimination in most situations, in discos and labour markets for example. There are always risks, but young people's opportunities and decisions still have lifelong implications. One's record when young still governs subsequent opportunities. Anyone hoping to reach the top of a management or professional career is still well advised to become as well qualified as possible when young, then embark quickly on the lower rungs of the appropriate career ladder. There is no guarantee that individuals who take these steps will rise even within reach of the career summits, but those who fail to take the initial steps can place themselves outside the fields.

What has disappeared is not the life course but the traditional life cycle in which successive cohorts followed one another through the same predictable and familiar sequences. These cyclical patterns have been replaced by a life course through which individuals take varied individualized routes. Each step influences future possibilities, but often in ways that could not have been predicted reliably in advance even in terms of useful statistical probabilities.

Policy implications

Guidance needs

One response to the individualization of young people's biographies and situations, and their need to take risks, has been to argue that these trends have increased their need for continuous individualized careers information, advice, and guidance. Standardized packages aimed at large groups of young people are said to be less useful than in the past. Young people's current need, it would appear from the preceding analysis, is for customized assistance that matches their particular circumstances. Delivering such a service in the traditional way, through career teachers and officers, would be prohibitively expensive, and, in any case, the demands would probably exceed the skills and knowledge that could be realistically expected of guidance personnel, but new technology could be a solution. Computers allow large quantities of continuously updated information to be stored and interrogated on a self-service basis according to individuals' specific circumstances and interests. The roles of career teachers and officers, therefore, may need to be redefined in terms of making their clients capable of putting themselves in charge.

Given that transitions have been prolonged and that the outcomes have become uncertain, it can be argued that answers to young people's career problems can no longer be couched as 'final solutions'— information about the particular occupations that they might enter which would best match their abilities and interests. Preparing young people for today's labour markets, it can be argued, means training them for life games involving mixtures of strategy and chance. Through career games that simulate real life situations young people may learn to take risks and decisions, and to reassess their strategies continuously in the light of the outcomes of earlier decisions and changing circumstances. These careers education implications do indeed appear to follow logically from the preceding analysis of how young people's situations are changing.

Without disputing the diagnosis, three qualifications are necessary. First, whatever information and guidance are offered by schools, the Careers Service and other official agencies, young people will probably continue to be most influenced by advice and information about the world of work obtained from parents, other family members, friends, and classroom teachers. Studies of school-leavers from the early twentieth century onwards have consistently found that members of young people's primary social networks have been more influential than official guidance personnel, and there are no reasons to believe that this situation will change. Secondly, no amount of information, advice, and guidance, however technically sophisticated, will eliminate risk and uncertainty from young people's lives. This goal is beyond the capabilities of guidance, just as, in earlier years, the impact of guidance was as constrained as young people's scope for choice by the surrounding opportunity structures. Thirdly, in the long term the way in which young people are most likely to learn to cope with their new condition is through its normalization.

Normalizing risk and uncertainty

In the 1940s and 50s there were fears that young people would find their abrupt transitions traumatic given the differences between the length of the school day and the working day in industry, the abrupt transfer from the most senior school classes to the most junior grades, the differences between the pastoral teacher and the amoral workplace supervisor, and so on. Actually all the relevant studies found that most school-leavers coped with their abrupt transitions with little difficulty. This was partly because they knew what to expect. They knew roughly what work would be like from listening to parents, older siblings, and neighbours. Equally to the point, the transition into employment was regarded as a normal event with which people had to cope. If young people manage to cope with prolonged transitions, uncertainty, and risk, this is likely to owe more to the normalization of these conditions than any forms of human or electronic careers guidance. In fact it can be argued that normalization is already well advanced.

Members of older generations who have experienced successful and continuous careers, just as they planned and expected when they were young, may pity today's youth. The latter inevitably see things rather differently (see Berger *et al.* 1993). Prolonged transitions are now taken for granted throughout most of Europe and North America. Today's 16-year-olds know that they will probably have to wait years before embarking on adult careers. This is the most likely significance of the emergence of the so-called *Generation X* of self-styled *slackers*. Young people who live for raves and appear relatively indifferent to their career situations are not refusing to conform so much as adapting and adjusting in the new condition that society has created for them.

Uncertain futures and risk taking are also becoming just parts of life for today's youth. This is not to say that many would not prefer greater security, more rapid transitions, and better jobs than are actually available. It is simply to note that these problems are now normal. In individualized societies people cannot have clearly bounded membership or reference groups, but young people cannot but be aware that most members of their generation share similar uncertain situations. Recognition that this situation is normal is all that is required to prevent individuals worrying that their own lives are in a hopeless mess. To repeat, this is not to suggest or imply that young people are enthusiastic about their new circumstances. The majority appear to retain hopes of progressive careers and stable marriages. Simultaneously, they seem able to cope with the realization that their futures may well be different from what they would have preferred.

Uncertainty can be threatening but it can also be liberating. The security of guaranteed futures can be comforting but also constraining. Some members of earlier generations rebelled and dropped out, albeit temporarily in most instances, from the predictable careers in dull bureaucracies, and family lives in 'little boxes', that apparently lay ahead. Since the 1970s young people's main concern has not been to 'break out' but to 'get in' (Braungart and Braungart 1986, 1990). This has become an international worry, but not necessarily or even usually a source of acute distress. The worry would not go away if young people were given more, better, and more continuous information and guidance from either counsellors or computers. Young people's concerns simply reflect the fact that there is no longer a secure and stable adult world for them to enter.

How great a change?

Given that entering employment has always given young people some reasons to worry, it may be queried whether we really need a new vocabulary to analyse their current predicaments. The originality of the terminology undoubtedly exaggerates the extent of change. We have seen that many important features of the transition have survived recent changes in education and the economy.

However, the new vocabulary of individualization, risk, and uncertainty can be defended as highlighting exactly what has changed. Most young people's transitions into the work-force have not been destroyed. Formerly disadvantaged young people have not seen their relative prospects improve. The vast majority of young people's desire and ability to work have not been eroded. However, there are now more persistent mismatches than rapid convergences between young people's career aspirations and their early career attainments, and this is just one manifestation of a broader constellation of changes. Seen in the context of labour markets where everyone's prospects have become uncertain, maintaining a distance between one's self and one's current position, whatever this might be, can be regarded as a highly functional mode of adjustment from the points of view of both individuals' well-being and the economy.

Flexible transition systems

All modern societies have replaced their earlier relatively rigid transition arrangements in which particular kinds of education and training fed into given sections of the labour market with more flexible systems. Modern transition systems need the same types of flexibility—numerical and functional—that are said to characterize post-Fordist firms. The systems need numerical flexibility so that they can cope with demographic highs and lows, ups and downs in labour demand, and the generally rising rather than falling levels of educational attainment and aspiration of young people and their parents. Numerical flexibility needs to be accompanied by functional flexibility, meaning that most types of education and training need to be capable of feeding into several sections of the labour market. This has become necessary in order to deal with unpredicted and often unpredictable changes in labour demand, and to handle the persistent mismatches between young people's ambitions and, therefore, the types of education, training, and qualifications that they seek, and the structure of labour demand.

Basing education and training provisions on labour demand forecasts does not work. The communist countries tried this type of planning and exposed its weaknesses. It is impossible to predict labour demand a decade or more ahead as would be necessary to bring appropriate programmes of education and training on stream. In planned systems it is also necessary to 'conscript' young people into prescribed forms of education and training, and in democracies there are more votes in providing the education and training that people want.

Every modern country's flexible transition system has been built on its own historically set pattern of education and training. So there are persistent differences between the countries of the United Kingdom, and more so across the European Union. These systems are not converging towards a point where their national characters will disappear; they are all simply becoming more flexible versions of their former selves.

This book has been consistently sceptical towards claims that the UK's methods of vocational preparation are less capable of delivering the workers required by a modern world class economy than education and training in other parts of Europe. If these criticisms of the UK's education and training were valid one would expect employers to be experiencing persistent difficulties in recruiting enough young people capable of being trained up to the standards that the firms require. There is in fact no evidence of any such widespread problem. There is far more evidence of young people being obliged to defer their entry into employment for longer than they would prefer, of them being unable to obtain jobs that match their qualifications, skills, and aspirations, and then facing working lives in which they will be underemployed relative to their proven capacities. If Britain's economy is weaker than its European and North American competitors' there are more likely explanations than deficiencies in the country's education and training. Likewise, if the countries of the old West are losing markets to competitors from the Pacific rim this seems more likely to be due to the latter's lower wage and labour costs than their superior education. In Britain and other European countries it is not transition arrangements that are proving weak points in otherwise sound socio-economic systems so much as the transition systems, and the young people who are in transition, who are bearing the burdens of weaknesses in other quarters.

The need for family support

All prolonged, flexible transition systems presume that young people will normally be housed and supported financially by their families. Recent quantitative and qualitative inquiries, reviewed in the previous chapter, have stressed the important roles of families for young people in post-compulsory education and training, and maybe especially during unemployment.

As transitions have lengthened and become more expensive, more of the costs have been transferred on to families. This has happened in all countries, not just in Britain. Some young people benefit enormously from the financial backing and socio-emotional support, and the job advice and information, that their parents and their contacts supply. Young people are severely disadvantaged when their families are unable or unwilling to provide this support, or when they have no families to depend on. Young people leaving local authority care in Britain have an appalling rate of failed transitions which often lead to unemployment, homelessness, crime, and judicial custody rather than self-supporting lifestyles based on employment (Royal Philanthropic Society 1994). Centrepoint, a central London voluntary agency which works with young people, most of whom are living apart from their families, has estimated that 30 per cent of its clients are from foster care and children's homes, whereas only 1 per cent of all children in Britain are in statutory care (Hutson and Liddiard 1994). Forty-five per cent of teenagers who leave home in Britain are provoked by arguments in their families, 26 per cent of which involve violence. In 52 per cent of all home-leaving cases the parents are divorced. The percentage leaving home is higher for teenagers living with step-parents than single parents (Bunting 1994). Present-day families are not all sufficiently strong to provide the support that the transition system presumes. Alternatives to the family, albeit less than wholly satisfactory alternatives, have been developed for the under-16s. After this age, for most practical purposes, there are no safety nets.

The need for quality jobs

All transition arrangements have their credibility undermined when substantial numbers of young people are unable to complete their transitions by entering adult jobs. In practice successful transitions depend on the availability not just of any jobs but quality jobs. This is not merely because most young people have a strong preference for 'quality'. Households need at least one and preferably more adults earning in good jobs if they are to support their children through prolonged transitions, and put aside enough to support themselves in the post-working life stage.

Economies that cannot generate enough quality jobs have inevitable difficulties in keeping young people in transit for as long as is necessary. What appear to be weaknesses in school-to-work transition arrangements often turn out to be more fundamental economic problems. The social systems of the old Western countries are producing more would-be workers, generally young people with good qualifications and modest or high aspirations, than can be accommodated in good jobs. The economic and social systems in Britain have been in this kind of disequilibrium since the 1970s and until this imbalance is cured many young people's transitions must inevitably end in failure. Some may become part of a new underclass. The most vulnerable individuals will be from the most disadvantaged backgrounds in terms of family structure, their parents' employment records, and the levels of unemployment in their localities. It is likely that their parents, schools, and teachers, and the young people themselves, will continue to be blamed. But the roots of the young people's problems really lie in the economy's failure to generate sufficient quality employment combined with the success of other groups in claiming the quality jobs that are available.

Further reading

Some of the new European thinking about youth's current condition is developed in the following Anglo-German studies: L. Chisholm, P. Buchner, H. H. Kruger, and P. Brown (eds.), (1990), *Childhood, Youth and Social Change: A Comparative Perspective*, Falmer, Basingstoke; and K. Evans and W. R. Heinz (eds.), (1994) *Becoming Adults in England and Germany*, Anglo-German Foundation, London.

References

ALLATT, P., and YEANDLE, S. M. (1991), *Youth Unemployment and the Family: Voices of Disordered Times*, Routledge, London.

ASHTON, D. N., and FIELD, D. (1976), *Young Workers*, Hutchinson, London.

—— and MAGUIRE, M. (1983), *The Vanishing Youth Labour Market*, Youthaid Occasional Paper 3, London.

—— —— (1986), *Young Adults in the Labour Market*, Department of Employment, Research Paper 55, London.

—— —— and GARLAND, V. (1982), *Youth in the Labour Market*, Research Paper 34, Department of Employment, London.

—— —— and SPILLSBURY, M. (1989), *Restructuring the Labour Market: The Implications for Youth*, Macmillan, London.

BANKS, M., BATES, I., BREAKWELL, G., BYNNER, J., EMLER, N., JAMIESON, L., and ROBERTS, K. (1992), *Careers and Identities*, Open University Press, Milton Keynes.

—— and ULLAH, P. (1988), *Youth Unemployment in the 1980s: Its Psychological Effects*, Croom Helm, London.

Bargaining Report (1986), 'Young workers' pay', Labour Research Department (May), 5–16.

BATES, I. (1993a), 'A job which is "Right for me"? Social class, gender and individualisation', in I. Bates and G. Riseborough (eds.), *Youth and Inequality*, Open University Press, Buckingham.

—— (1993b), 'When I have my own studio. . . . The making and shaping of designer careers', in I. Bates and G. Riseborough, (eds.), *Youth and Inequality*, Open University Press, Buckingham.

—— CLARKE, J., COHEN, P., FINN, D., MOORE R., and WILLIS, P. (1984), *Schooling for the Dole*, Macmillan, London.

—— and RISEBOROUGH, G. (eds.), (1993), *Youth and Inequality*, Open University Press, Buckingham.

BAXTER, J. L. (1975), 'The chronic job-changer: a study of youth unemployment', *Social and Economic Administration*, 9: 184–206.

BECK, U. (1992), *Risk Society: Towards a New Modernity*, Sage, London.

BECKER, H. S., and CARPER, J. W. (1956a), 'The development of identification with an occupation', *American Journal of Sociology*, 61: 289–98.

—— —— (1956b), 'The elements of identification with an occupation', *American Sociological Review*, 21: 341–8.

—— —— (1957), 'Adjustments to conflicting expectations in the development of identification with an occupation', *Social Forces*, 36: 51–6.

BEETHAM, D. (1967), *Immigrant School-Leavers and the Youth Employment Service in Birmingham*, Institute of Race Relations, London.

References

BENNETT, R., GLENNERSTER H., and NEVISON, D. (1992a), 'Investing in Skill: to stay on or not to stay on', *Oxford Review of Economic Policy*, 8, 130–45.

—— —— —— (1992b), *Investing in Skill: Expected Returns to Vocational Studies*, Discussion Paper WSP/83, London School of Economics.

BERG, I. (1973), *Education and Jobs*, Penguin, Harmondsworth.

BERGER, P. A., STEINMULLER, P., and SOPP, P. (1993), 'Differentiation of life courses? Changing patterns of labour market sequences in West Germany', *European Sociological Review*, 9: 43–61.

BLACKMAN, S. J. (1987), 'The labour market in school: the new vocationalism and issues of socially ascribed discrimination', in P. Brown and D. N. Ashton (eds.), *Education, Unemployment and Labour Markets*, Falmer Press, Lewes.

BOWLES S., and GINTIS, H. (1976), *Schooling in Capitalist America*, Routledge, London.

BRAUNGART, R. G., and BRAUNGART, M. M. (1986), 'Youth problems and politics in the 1980s: some multinational comparisons', *International Sociology*, 1: 358–80.

—— —— (1990), 'Youth movements in the 1980s: a global perspective', *International Sociology*, 5: 157–81.

BRAVERMAN, H. (1974), *Labour and Monopoly Capital*, Monthly Review Press, New York.

BROWN, P. (1987), *Schooling Ordinary Kids: Inequality, Unemployment and the New Vocationalism*, Tavistock, London.

BUCHMANN, M., and CHARLES, M. (1992), 'Organisational and institutional determinants of women's labour force options: comparing six European countries', paper presented to First European Conference of Sociology, Vienna.

BUNTING, M. (1994), 'The abandoned generation', *Guardian* (1 June) 18.

BUSHELL, R. (1986), 'Evaluation of the Young Workers Scheme', *Employment Gazette* (May), 145–52.

BYNNER, J., and ROBERTS, K. (1991), *Youth and Work*, Anglo-German Foundation, London.

CAMERON, C., LUSH, A., and MEARA, G. (1943), *Disinherited Youth*, Carnegie Trust, Edinburgh.

CASSELS, J. (1990), *Britain's Real Skill Shortage*, Policy Studies Institute, London.

CHANDLER, J., and Wallace, C. (1990), 'Some alternatives in youth training: franchise and corporatist models', in D. Gleeson (ed.), *Training and its Alternatives*, Open University Press, Milton Keynes.

CHISHOLM, L., and DU BOIS-RAYMOND, M. (1993), 'Youth transitions: gender and social change', *Sociology*, 27: 259–79.

CLARK, B. R. (1960), 'The cooling-out function in higher education', *American Journal of Sociology*, 65: 569–76.

CLOUGH, E., and DREW, D. (1985), *Futures in Black and White*, Sheffield Polytechnic.

COCKBURN, C. (1987), *Two-Track Training: Sex Inequalities and the YTS*, Macmillan, London.

—— (1991), *In the Way of Women*, Macmillan, London.

COFFIELD, F. (1992), 'Training and Enterprise Councils: the last throw of voluntarism?', *Policy Studies*, 13/4, 11–32.

—— BORRILL, C., and MARSHALL, S. (1986), *Growing up at the Margins*, Open University Press, Milton Keynes.

CONNOLLY, M., ROBERTS, K., BEN-TOVIM, G., and TORKINGTON, P. (1991), *Black Youth in Liverpool*, Giordano Bruno, Culemborg.

CRAINE, S. F. (1994), 'Beggars Can't Be Choosers: An Ethnography of Post-School Transitions in a High Unemployment Area', Ph.D. thesis, University of Salford.

CROMPTON, R., and SANDERSON, K. (1986), 'Credentials and careers', *Sociology*, 20, 25–42.

CROSS, M., and SMITH, D. I. (eds.) (1987), *Black Youth Futures*, National Youth Bureau, Leicester.

CSIKSZENTMIHALYI, M. (1990), *Flow: The Psychology of Optional Experience*, Harper & Row, New York.

DAWS, P. (1977), *Social Determinism or Personal Choice?*, Studies in the Sociology of Vocational Guidance 1, University of Keele.

DENCH, S. (1993), 'What types of people are employers seeking to employ?', paper presented to Employment Department/Policy Studies Institute Conference on Unemployment in Focus, Rotherham.

Department of Education and Science (1979), *A Better Start in Working Life*, London.

Department of Trade and Industry (1994), *Competitiveness: Helping Business to Win*, HMSO, London.

DONOVAN, A., and ODDY, M. (1982), 'Psychological aspects of unemployment: an investigation into the emotional and social adjustment of school-leavers', *Journal of Adolescence*, 5: 15–30.

DORE, R. (1976), *The Diploma Disease*, Allen & Unwin, London.

DRIVER, G. (1980), 'How West Indians do better at school (especially the girls)', *New Society* (17 Jan.).

EKINSMYTH, C., and BYNNER, J. (1994), *The Basic Skills of Young Adults*, Adult Literacy and Basic Skills Unit, London.

ELDER, G. H. (1974), *Children of the Great Depression*, University of Chicago Press, Chicago.

Employment Department (1992), *Training Credits: A Report on the First 12 Months*, London.

—— (1993), *Labour Market and Skill Trends 1994/95*, London.

ERIKSON, R., and GOLDTHORPE, J. H. (1992), *The Constant Flux: A. Study of Class Mobility in Industrial Societies*, Clarendon Press, Oxford.

EVANS, K., and HEINZ, W. R. (eds.), (1994), *Becoming Adults in England and Germany*, Anglo-German Foundation, London.

EVANS, S. T. (1989), 'Uncovering socialisation processes at discotheques', paper presented to ESRC 16–19 Workshop, Sheffield.

EVETTS, J. (1992), 'Dimensions of career: avoiding reification in the analysis of change', *Sociology*, 26: 1–21.

FELSTEAD, A. (1993), *Putting Individuals in Charge, Leaving Skills Behind?*, Discussion Paper 5 93/9, Department of Sociology, University of Leicester.

References

FINN, D. (1987), *Training without Jobs*, Macmillan, London.

FLUDE, R. A., and WHITESIDE, M. T. (1971), 'Occupational identity, commitment to a trade and attitude to non–vocational courses amongst a group of craft apprentices', *Vocational Aspect*, 23: 69–72.

FULLER, M. (1980), 'Black girls in a London comprehensive school', in R. Deem (ed.), *Schooling for Women's Work*, Routledge, London.

FURLONG, A. (1992), *Growing up in a Classless Society?*, Edinburgh University Press, Edinburgh.

GALLIE, D., and WHITE, M. (1993), *Employee Commitment and the Skills Revolution*, Policy Studies Institute, London.

GARNER, C., MAIN, G. M. B., and RAFFE, D. (1988), 'A tale of four cities: social and spatial inequalities in the youth labour market', in D. Raffe (ed.), *Education and the Youth Labour Market*, Falmer Press, Lewes.

GEER, B. (ed.) (1972), *Learning to Work*, Russell Sage, New York.

GOLDTHORPE, J. H., LLEWELLYN, C., and PAYNE, C. (1987), *Social Mobility and Class Structure in Modern Britain*, Clarendon Press, Oxford.

GRAY, J., JESSON, D., and SIME, N. (1992), 'The "discouraged worker" revisited: post-16 participation in education south of the border', *Sociology*, 26: 493–505.

GREAVES, K. (1983), *The Youth Opportunities Programme in Contrasting Local Areas*, Manpower Services Commission Research and Development Series 16, Sheffield.

GRIFFIN, C. (1985), *Typical Girls?* Routledge, London.

HAWORTH, J. T. (1993), 'Skill challenge relationships and psychological well-being in everyday life', *Society and Leisure*, 16: 115–128.

HENDRY, L. B., RAYMOND, M., and STEWART, C. (1984), 'Unemployment, school and leisure: an adolescent study', *Leisure Studies*, 3: 175–87.

HILL, J. M. M., and SCHARFF, D. E. (1976), *Between Two Worlds*, Careers Consultants, London.

HOLT, M. (ed.) (1987), *Skills and Vocationalism: The Easy Answer*, Open University Press, Milton Keynes.

HUNT, J., and SMALL, P. (1981), *Employing Young People*, Scottish Council for Research in Education, Edinburgh.

HUTSON, S. (1992), *Saturday Jobs: Part-Time Working by Young People 16–18 Years in Full-Time Education*, end of award report 000231510, ESRC, Swindon.

—— and CHEUNG, W. (1991), 'Saturday jobs: sixth formers in the labour market and the family', in C. Marsh and S. Arber (eds.), *Family and Household: Division and Change*, Macmillan, London.

—— and JENKINS, R. (1989), *Taking the Strain*, Open University Press, Milton Keynes.

—— and LIDDIARD, M. (1994), *Youth Homelessness*, Macmillan, Basingstoke.

IFF Research (1990), *Skill Needs in Britain*, London.

—— (1993), *Small Firms' Skill Needs and Training Survey*, London.

ISTANCE, D., REES, G., and WILLIAMSON, H. (1994), *Young People Not in Education, Training or Employment in South Glamorgan*, South Glamorgan Training and Enterprise Council, Cardiff.

JACKSON, P. R., and STAFFORD, E. M. (1980), 'Work involvement and employment status as influences on mental health', paper presented to British Psychological Society, Canterbury.

JARVIS V., and PRAIS, S. J. (1988), 'Two nations of shopkeepers: training for retailing in France and Britain', Discussion Paper 140, National Institute of Economic and Social Research, London.

JENKINS, R. (1982), 'Acceptability, suitability and the search for the habituated worker: how ethnic minorities and women lose out', paper presented to Workshop on the Management and Mismanagement of Labour, Loughborough University.

JONES, T. (1993), *Britain's Ethnic Minorities*, Policy Studies Institute, London.

JUNAKAR, P. N. (ed.), (1987), *From School to Unemployment: The Labour Market for Young People*, Macmillan, London.

KEIL, T., FORD, J., BRYMAN, A., and BEARDSWORTH, A. (1982), 'Does occupational status matter? The case of recruitment', paper presented to Workshop on the Management and Mismanagement of Labour, Loughborough University.

Labour Market Quarterly Report (1993), 'YT outcomes', Employment Department, Sheffield (Aug.).

LAYARD, R. (1992), *The Training Reform Act of 1994*, annual lecture 1992, ESRC, Swindon.

LAYDER, D., ASHTON, D., and SUNG, J. (1991), 'The empirical correlates of action and structure: the transition from school to work', *Sociology*, 25: 447–64.

LEE, D. J., MARSDEN, D., RICKMAN, P., and DUNCOMBE, J. (1989), *Scheming for Youth: A Study of YTS in the Enterprise Culture*, Open University Press, Milton Keynes.

LIVOCK, R. (1983), *Screening in the Recruitment of Young Workers*, Department of Employment Research Paper 41, London.

LONEY, M. (1979), 'The politics of job creation', in G. Craig, M. Mayo, and N. Sharman, (eds.), *Jobs and Community Action*, Routledge, London.

MACDONALD, R., and COFFIELD, F. (1991), *Risky Business? Youth and the Enterprise Culture*, Falmer Press, Lewes.

—— —— (1993), 'Young people and training credits: an early exploration', *British Journal of Education and Work*, 6: 5–21.

MCPHERSON, A., and WILLMS, J. D. (1987), 'Equalisation and improvement: some effects of comprehensive re-organisation in Scotland', *Sociology*, 21: 509–39.

MCRAE, S., DEVINE, F., and LAKEY, J. (1991), *Women into Engineering and Science*, Policy Studies Institute, London.

MAKEHAM, P. (1980), *Youth Unemployment*, Research Paper 11, Department of Employment, London.

Manpower Services Commission (1977), *Young People at Work*, London.

—— (1981a), *A New Training Initiative: A Consultative Document*, London.

—— (1981b), *A New Training Initiative: an Agenda for Action*, London.

MANWARING, T. (1982), 'The extended internal labour market', paper presented to Workshop on the Management and Mismanagement of Labour, Loughborough University.

References

MASON, G., and VAN ARK, B. (1993), *Productivity, Machinery and Skills in Engineering: An Anglo-Dutch Comparison*, Discussion Paper 36, National Institute of Economic and Social Research, London.

MERTON, R. K., READER, G. G., and KENDALL, P. L. (eds.) (1957), *The Student Physician*, Harvard University Press.

MIRZA, H. S. (1992), *Young, Female and Black*, Routledge, London.

MURRAY, C. (1990), *The Emerging British Underclass*, Institute of Economic Affairs, London.

National Curriculum Council (1991), *Work Experience and the School Curriculum*, York.

National Economic Development Office (1988), *Young People and the Labour Market: A Challenge for the 1990s*, London.

PARK, A. (1994), *England and Wales Youth Cohort Survey: Young People 18–19 Years Old in 1991*, Youth Cohort Series 29, Employment Department, Sheffield.

PARKER, H. (1974), *A View from the Boys*, David & Charles, Newton Abbot.

PAYNE, J. (1987), 'Does unemployment run in families?', *Sociology*, 21: 199–214.

PENHALE, B. (1989), 'Associations between unemployment and fertility among young women in the early 1980s', Working Paper 60, Social Statistics Research Unit, City University, London.

PIKE, G., CONNOR, H., and JAGGER, N. (1992), *IMS Graduate Review 1992*, Institute of Manpower Studies, University of Sussex.

PRAIS, S. J., and WAGNER, K. (1985), 'Schooling standards in England and Germany: some summary comparisons bearing on economic performance', *National Institute Economic Review*, 112 (May): 53–73.

RAFFE, D. (1985), *Youth Unemployment in the UK 1979–84*, Centre for Educational Sociology, Edinburgh.

—— (1987), 'The context of the Youth Training Scheme: an analysis of its strategy and development', *British Journal of Education and Work*, 1: 1–33.

—— (1988), 'Going with the grain: youth training in transition', in S. Brown and R. Wake, (eds.), *Education in Transition*, Scottish Council for Research in Education, Edinburgh.

—— and COURTENAY, G. (1988), '16–18 on both sides of the border', in D. Raffe (ed.), *Education and the Youth Labour Market*, Falmer Press, Lewes.

—— and WILLMS, J. D. (1989), 'Schooling the discouraged worker: local labour market effects on education participation', *Sociology*, 23: 559–81.

RAGGATT, P. (1988), 'Quality control in the dual system of West Germany', *Oxford Review of Education*, 14: 163–86.

RAJAN, A. (1985), *Job Subsidies: Do They Work?*, Institute of Manpower Studies, University of Sussex.

RAWSTRON, E. M., and COATES, B. E. (1966), 'Opportunity and affluence', *Geography*, 51: 1–15.

REES, T. L., and ATKINSON, P. (eds.), (1982), *Youth Unemployment and State Intervention*, Routledge, London.

RISEBOROUGH, G. (1993*a*), 'Learning a living or living a learning? An ethnography of BTEC National Diploma students', in I. Bates and G. Riseborough, (eds.), *Youth and Inequality*, Open University Press, Buckingham.

—— (1993*b*), 'GBH—the Gobbo Barmy Harmy: one day in the life of the YTS boys', in I. Bates and G. Riseborough (eds.), *Youth and Inequality*, Open University Press, Buckingham.

RISKOWSKI, G. (1993), *Working for Leisure?*, Epping Forest College, Epping.

Robbins Report (1963), *Higher Education*, Committee on Higher Education, HMSO, London.

ROBERTS, K. (1967), 'The incidence and effects of spare-time employment amongst schoolchildren', *Vocational Aspect*, 11: 129–36.

—— (1968), 'The entry into employment: an approach towards a general theory', *Sociological Review*, 16: 165–84.

—— (1975), 'The developmental theory of occupational choice: a critique and an alternative', in G. Esland *et al.* (eds.), *People and Work*, Holme McDougall, Edinburgh.

—— (1977), 'The social conditions, consequences and limitations of careers guidance', *British Journal of Guidance and Counselling*, 5: 1–9.

—— (1993), 'Career trajectories and the mirage of increased social mobility', in I. Bates and G. Riseborough (eds.), *Youth and Inequality*, Open University Press, Buckingham.

—— CAMPBELL, R., and FURLONG, A. (1990), 'Class and gender divisions among young adults at leisure', in C. Wallace and M. Cross (eds.), *Youth in Transition*, Falmer Press, London.

—— and CHADWICK, C. (1991), *Transitions into the Labour Market: The New Routes of the 1980s*, Youth Cohort Series 16, Research and Development Series 65, Employment Department, Sheffield.

—— CLARK, S. C., and WALLACE, C. (1994), 'Flexibility and individualisation: a comparison of transitions into employment in England and Germany', *Sociology*, 28: 31–54.

—— and CORCORAN-NANTES, Y. (1994), 'TQM, the new training and industrial relations', in A. Wilkinson and H. Willmott (eds.), *Making Quality Critical*, Routledge, London.

—— —— (1995), 'We've got one of those', *Gender, Work and Organization*, 2.

—— DENCH, S., and RICHARDSON, D. (1986), 'Firms' uses of the Youth Training Scheme', *Policy Studies*, 6: 37–53.

—— —— —— (1987), *The Changing Structure of Youth Labour Markets*, Department of Employment Research Paper 59, London.

—— DUGGAN, J., and NOBLE, M. (1981), *Unregistered Youth Unemployment and Outreach Careers Work, Part I, Non-registration*, Research Paper 31, Department of Employment, London.

—— NOBLE, M., and DUGGAN, J. (1982), 'Youth unemployment: an old problem or a new life-style?' *Leisure Studies*, 1: 171–82.

—— and PARSELL, G. (1991), 'Young people's sources and levels of income, and patterns of consumption in Britain in the late-1980s', *Youth and Policy*, 35 (Dec.): 20–5.

References

ROBERTS, K., and PARSELL, G. (1992*a*), 'The stratification of Youth Training', *British Journal of Education and Work*, 5: 65–83.

—— —— (1992*b*), 'Entering the labour market in Britain: the survival of traditional opportunity structures', *Sociological Review*, 30: 727–53.

—— —— and CONNOLLY, M. (1991), 'Young people's transitions into the labour market', in M. Cross and G. Payne (eds.), *Work and the Enterprise Culture*, Falmer Press, London.

ROSE, R., and PAGE, E. C. (1989), *Searching and Acting in Adversity*, Centre for the Study of Public Policy No. 174, University of Strathclyde.

Royal Philanthropic Society (1994), *Leaving Care in the 1990s*, Westerham, Kent.

RYRIE, A. C., and WEIR, A. D. (1978), *Getting a Trade*, Hodder & Stoughton, London.

SARGANT, N. (1993), *Learning for a Purpose*, National Institute of Adult Continuing Education, Leicester.

SAUNDERS, P. (1994), 'Is Britain a meritocracy', in R. M. Blackburn (ed.), *Social Inequality in a Changing World*, Sociological Research Group, Cambridge.

Schools Council Inquiry, 1 (1968), *Young School-Leavers*, HMSO, London.

SHACKLETON, J. R. (1993), 'Investing in training: questioning the conventional wisdom', *Policy Studies*, 14/3: 29–40.

SHANKS, K. (1982), *After Community Industry*, Community Industry, London.

SMITH, D. V., and SUGARMAN, L. (1981), 'An evaluation of the government's Work Experience programme for the young unemployed', *British Journal of Guidance and Counselling*, 9: 65–73.

SMITHERS, A. (1993), *All our Futures: Britain's Educational Revolution*, Channel 4 Television, London.

STEEDMAN, H. (1988), 'Vocational education and manufacturing employment in Western Europe', National Institute of Economic and Social Research, London, unpublished paper.

Swann Report (1985), *Education for All*, Committee of Inquiry into the Education of Children from Ethnic Minority Groups, HMSO, London.

TRAVERS, P. (1986), 'Contingent and noncontingent effects of unemployment', *Sociology*, 20: 192–206.

WALLACE, C. D. (1987), *For Richer, for Poorer*, Tavistock, London.

WEINER, M. J. (1981), *English Culture and the Decline of the Industrial Spirit*, Cambridge University Press, Cambridge.

WELLS, W. (1983), *The Relative Pay and Employment of Young People*, Research Paper 42, Department of Employment, London.

WEST, M., and NEWTON, P. (1983), *The Transition from School to Work*, Croom Helm, London.

WHITE, M., and McRAE, S. (1989), *Young Adults and Long-Term Unemployment*, Policy Studies Institute, London.

WILLIS, P. (1977), *Learning to Labour*, Saxon House, Farnborough.

—— BEKEM, A., ELLIS, T., and WHITT, D. (1988), *The Youth Review: Social Conditions of Young People in Wolverhampton*, Avebury, Aldershot.

ZINNEKER, J. (1990), 'What does the future hold? Youth and socio-cultural change in the FRG', in L. Chisholm, P. Buchner, H. H. Kruger, and P. Brown (eds.), *Childhood, Youth and Social Change: A Comparative Perspective*, Falmer, Basingstoke.

Index

Index